BLESSED
ASSURANCE

BIBLE BOOKSHELF

*T*he book in your hand is the fourth in an exciting new series of Sabbath school lesson supplements. Based on the ten-year cycle of Sabbath school lessons, this set will eventually form a forty-volume commentary on the entire Bible. Many of the church's best-known Biblical scholars and authors are contributing to this series.

Start now to collect the entire Bible Bookshelf set. It's an easy, inexpensive way to build your own Biblical reference library. The first three volumes are still available at your Adventist Book Center.

In the Beginning, by Arthur J. Ferch (Genesis)

Meet Pastor Peter, by Bernard E. Seton (2 Peter, Jude)

Prison Papers From a Captive Ambassador, by Mario Veloso (Ephesians)

The Bible Bookshelf series is a joint project of the Review and Herald and Pacific Press publishing associations.

BLESSED
ASSURANCE

WILLIAM G. JOHNSSON

REVIEW AND HERALD PUBLISHING ASSOCIATION
Washington, DC 20039-0555
Hagerstown, MD 21740

Copyright © 1985 by
Review and Herald Publishing Association

This book was
Edited by Richard W. Coffen
Designed by Richard Steadham
Cover photos by The Image Bank (large); Mennonite
Information Center, Lancaster, PA full size reproduction of
Jewish sanctuary Ark of the Covenant detail (inset)
Type set: 11/12 Zapf

PRINTED IN U.S.A.

To Bob and Ellen—

good neighbors, best friends

Contents

Introduction

Habakkuk and Hebrews are neglected books of the Bible. The former is usually lost amid the small prophetic books that close out the Old Testament; the latter discourages many readers because it seems to be laden with heavy theology and involved reasoning.

But the sincere seeker for truth will find both books deeply rewarding. They speak to men and women today in a manner that often is startling, raising the questions *we* are asking, and wrestling with the doubts *we* face. And they show us what we all seek—the path to confident, buoyant living in Jesus Christ.

Studied together, Habakkuk and Hebrews shed light on each other, for the way to assurance is the same whether people live six hundred years before Jesus or 1,900 years after Him.

Blessed Assurance is divided into thirteen short chapters that correspond with the lessons for the Sabbath school quarterly *In Full Assurance*. Each chapter takes two or three of the main ideas outlined in the Sabbath School lesson and develops them. The book can be read and studied without reference to the Sabbath school quarterly. However, it does not regurgitate the material of the lessons, so the serious Bible student will find maximum benefit by studying this book in conjunction with the quarterly.

"Let us draw near with a true heart in full assurance of faith," admonishes the writer of Hebrews (chap. 10:22). May his counsel be realized in everyone who reads *Blessed Assurance.*

A Believer's Questions

[Hab. 1:1-2:4]

A story making the rounds of academia sometime ago told of a psychology professor who was giving the final examination for his class. He walked into the classroom, wrote a question on the chalkboard, and strode out. The question: "Why?"

An examination like that deserves an answer in kind. While the rest of the class scratched their heads and eventually labored to produce several pages, one student wrote "Because" and turned in her paper.

She earned an A!

The fact is, that little word *why* is the most common of all the questions that confront modern people—and also the most troubling. Often there doesn't seem to be any "because."

Which leads us to Habakkuk, an obscure writer who lived about six hundred years before Jesus but who asks the very questions men and women pose today. He asks *our* questions. His book has a contemporary ring about it. And that's why the "because" he found can affect our lives also.

We read his dialogue with God in the opening portion of his book, chapter 1:1-2:4. The passage asks startling questions of God. But it also shows us how a *believer* handles doubt and what it means to live by faith.

Startling Questions

"O Lord, how long shall I cry for help, and thou wilt not hear? Or cry to thee 'Violence!' and thou wilt not save? Why dost thou make me see wrongs and look upon trouble?

Destruction and violence are before me; strife and conten-
tion arise. So the law is slacked and justice never goes forth.
For the wicked surround the righteous, so justice goes forth
perverted" (Hab. 1:2-4).

Why doesn't God answer? In the twentieth century men
and women are oppressed by the silence of God. Of course,
every century, including Habakkuk's, has grappled with
God's seeming unresponsiveness, but in ours the silence
has assumed thunder proportions.

Think of the twentieth century—the wisest and weakest
of all time:

● two catastrophic global wars that killed scores of
millions and maimed as many others. When the bombs fall,
not just the soldiers suffer: babies and grandfathers,
pregnant women and handicapped people, are exposed
and vulnerable.

● 6 million people were wiped out in a systematic
campaign of annihilation, Hitler's "final solution" to the
problem of the Jews.

● acts of barbarism and terrorism have become part of the
daily news. The Idi Amins, the car bomb terrorists, the IRA,
and others of their ilk carry out monstrous deeds of murder
and destruction.

When the bombs fall, where is God?

Where was God at Auschwitz?

Where was God when the methyl isocyanate gas escaped
from the Union Carbide Corporation plant in Bhopal, India,
spreading a cloud of death and torture over the poor of the
city, killing more than two thousand people, and injuring
multitudes?

Where is God in the parched Sahel and in East Africa as
half a million Ethiopians starve to death and as the millions
of babies who survive face lives of permanent mental
retardation?

Why doesn't God answer? This is the terrible question of
the late twentieth century. It is the question that, after
Auschwitz, has robbed millions of Jews of their ancestral
faith and made our times the age of unbelief.

After all, if God could bring the world into existence simply by speaking, if He could roll back the waters of the Red Sea, couldn't He make it rain on the drought-stricken parts of Africa? Couldn't He have shut off the valve to prevent the methyl isocyanate gas from escaping?

Why all this violence? Violence is a blot on American society. Despite all the money spent to provide free education, our streets remain unsafe, and we have to lock ourselves in with chains, deadbolts, electric burglar alarms, and German shepherds. We can put men on the moon, but we can't get criminals off the street!

Violence takes many forms. The most appalling, perhaps, is the abuse of the innocent, the aged, and the defenseless. Today even nuns and 80-year-old women are raped. Children are exploited for pornographic movies. Hundreds of thousands of youngsters are sexually abused by relatives. And untold numbers of women suffer in silence the battering of their bodies and the indignities to their person—all to satisfy perverted male egos and appetites.

In fact—and this is perhaps the saddest commentary—violence *sells*. It sells TV programs, movies, children's cartoons, even sports. The grim truth is that people love to experience it vicariously.

Are we any better than Rome with her Colosseum?

Why this lack of righteousness? Every Sunday 50 to 60 million people in North America go to church. The Gallup survey shows an increased interest in religion. Between 40 and 50 million men and women claim to have been "born again." But these statistics are deceptive. Religious profession doesn't equal righteous living. The reality is that America is on a moral toboggan slide.

Take cheating, for instance. On TV popular characters lie and cheat. In real life children cheat on their tests. Students cheat even at West Point. Men cheat on their wives. Wives cheat on their husbands. And both cheat the IRS.

For too many, religion has the form but denies the power. The moral fiber of society has rotted away, eaten up by the "fast buck" and "if it feels right, it must be right" type of philosophy.

Capital punishment, it is said, means that if you have the capital you don't get the punishment. Tax loopholes, legal loopholes, legislative loopholes, provide a way to get by the law—and morality. And meanwhile the underground economy—the tax-free world of the Mafia, the drug dealers, the vice ring, the gamblers—flourishes.

Why doesn't God answer? Why all this violence? Why this lack of righteousness? These are *our* questions.

But first they were a believer's questions—Habakkuk's. And he also will give us help in our search for answers.

How to Handle Doubt

1. *Habakkuk was a believer before he was a questioner.* This is the first point we must keep in mind. It was *because* Habakkuk was a believer that he became a questioner. He had such a high view of God that he couldn't understand how God, who had acted so mightily in Israel's past, could be silent when violence, oppression, and lawlessness were abounding. Nor could he fathom how God, in response to his first set of questions, could propose to use the pagan Babylonians as agents of His punishment (Hab. 1:5-17).

Believers and skeptics may address the same questions to God, but their attitudes are vastly different. Skeptics ask in order to challenge God, to mock His existence or His power, to justify their own unbelieving course of life. But believers ask because they care about God and the honor of His name, because they seek to understand His ways.

A very old definition of theology, formulated by Anselm, archbishop of Canterbury in the eleventh century, is "faith seeking understanding." We believe in order that we may understand; we do not seek to understand in order that we may believe.

2. *Habakkuk was honest with God and with himself.* There was no phoniness about Habakkuk—no effort to give pat answers, to dispense the kind of theological Pablum that the court prophets, or perhaps even his fellow singers in the Temple choir (for he was a singer and composer; see chap.

3:19), would approve.

Habakkuk didn't take his questions to his fellows. He didn't go about sowing doubts among the people. He took his questions to God.

3. *Habakkuk was prepared to wait for God to answer.* "I will take my stand to watch, and station myself on the tower, and look forth to see what he will say to me, and what I will answer concerning my complaint," he said (chap. 2:1).

The failure with many of our prayers is that we give up too soon. We don't give God a chance. We forget that prayer is a two-way street, a *communion* with God. As children of the "instant" generation we want instant answers. But some answers don't come, can't come, as quickly as we wish.

God doesn't keep us waiting for answers because He likes to see us standing at the door, hat in hand. In fact, the delay doesn't come from Him at all—it comes from us. God can't give us the answers we need until we are ready to receive them.

"Prayer is the opening of the heart to God as to a friend. Not that it is necessary, in order to make known to God what we are, but in order to enable us to receive Him. Prayer does not bring God down to us, but brings us up to Him." "If we take counsel with our doubts and fears, or try to solve everything that we cannot see clearly, before we have faith, perplexities will only increase and deepen. But if we come to God, feeling helpless and dependent, as we really are, and in humble, trusting faith make known our wants to Him whose knowledge is infinite, who sees everything in creation, and who governs everything by His will and word, He can and will attend to our cry, and will let light shine into our hearts. Through sincere prayer we are brought into connection with the mind of the Infinite. We may have no remarkable evidence at the time that the face of our Redeemer is bending over us in compassion and love; but this is even so. We may not feel His visible touch, but His hand is upon us in love and pitying tenderness."—*Steps to Christ*, pp. 93, 96, 97.

Today, most people are long on doubts. Could the reason be that they are short on prayer?

4. *Habakkuk, in the midst of doubts, recalled God's leading in the past.* Although he could not grasp how the Lord could adopt the idolatrous Babylonians as His means of judgment on Israel, he nevertheless could say, "Art thou not from everlasting, O Lord my God, my Holy One? We shall not die" (chap. 1:12).

Habakkuk knew God, knew Him personally, not just as a theory. He knew of God's saving deeds in days of old, when He had rescued Israel from the brink of destruction—such as when the army of Sennacherib, surrounding Jerusalem, was decimated overnight (see Isa. 37:33-37). God, the Everlasting One, was *his* God, and Israel's God. As He had saved the nation in the past, He also would bring them through the Babylonian scourge, bitter though that would be.

Other Bible characters likewise found strength and hope through similar recall. Job, broken in body and buffeted by "friends" and doubts, cast his mind back to the years of the Lord's blessing. David, a fugitive from his own people and returning to his adopted home to find the city razed and his family carried off, "strengthened himself in the Lord his God" as his own men muttered plots of revolt (1 Sam. 30:6).

And Jesus, in the agony of forsakenness, uttered the cry of dereliction first voiced by the psalmist: " 'My God, my God, why hast thou forsaken me?' " (Ps. 22:1; Matt. 27:46). In His pain, did He recall how the psalm ends? "For he hath not despised nor abhorred the affliction of the afflicted; neither hath he hid his face from him; but when he cried unto him, he heard. My praise shall be of thee in the great congregation: I will pay my vows before them that fear him" (Ps. 22:24, 25, K.J.V.).

Ellen White underscores the same point. In the chapter "What to Do With Doubt" in *Steps to Christ* she reminds the questioner: "There is an evidence that is open to all—the most highly educated, and the most illiterate—the evidence of experience."—Page 111. And if we should tremble as we confront the future, she encourages us: "We have nothing to fear for the future, except as we shall forget the way the Lord has led us, and His teaching in our past history."—*Life Sketches*, p. 196.

The Life of Faith

Now we can better appreciate the climactic verse of the dialogue between Habakkuk and God. After the prophet, torn by questions, has resolved to wait for the Lord's answers, he hears the certainty of the divine purposes and then this word: "The just shall live by his faith" (Hab. 2:4, K.J.V.).

The word *faith* here, in Hebrew *enûmâh*, connotes *faithfulness*. Modern translations bring out this meaning: "Behold, he whose soul is not upright in him shall fail, but the righteous shall live by his faithfulness" (verse 4, margin). " 'See, he is puffed up; his desires are not upright—but the righteous will live by his faith' " (N.I.V.).

The Christian life is more than a decision for Christ at a point in time. It is far more than a warm feeling, a glow of emotion. It is more than mouthing clichés and platitudes. Christianity means trusting God in the darkness as well as in the light, in suffering as in happiness. It means holding on to Him, refusing to let go His hand even though we are at our wits' end. " 'I will not let you go, unless you bless me' " (Gen. 32:26)—this is the life of faith.

Said the great apostle to the Gentiles, he who had suffered beatings, shipwreck, imprisonment, false accusations, and the burden of caring for the infant churches: "We are afflicted in every way, but not crushed; perplexed, but not driven to despair; persecuted, but not forsaken; struck down, but not destroyed; always carrying in the body the death of Jesus, so that the life of Jesus may also be manifested in our bodies. For while we live we are always being given up to death for Jesus' sake, so that the life of Jesus may be manifested in our mortal flesh" (2 Cor. 4:8-11).

Does reason have a part in the life of faith? Indeed. God calls us to the use of every capacity, for His glory. This, He says, is our "reasonable service" (Rom. 12:1, 2, K.J.V.).

In this age of unbelief, rational arguments can—and

should—be advanced for the existence of God. The evidence of design in nature, for example, suggests the existence of a Designer.

In Biblical religion, faith and reason complement each other. The Scriptures are indissolubly bound up with history—with God's saving acts in the Old Testament and His supreme act in the New. Decision for Christ is not a leap in the dark (although it is a leap). It presupposes a basis of knowledge about Jesus of Nazareth, a Jew of the first century whom Christians aver to have been God incarnate. Faith ultimately goes beyond reason, however. Its knowledge is more than historical; it is experiential. Faith *knows* God. Like Habakkuk it can say, "O Lord *my* God, *my* Holy One" (Hab. 1:12).

For this reason believers can live without solutions to all their problems. In large measure the ways of God remain mysterious to us, but we have *sufficient* answers. Habakkuk found them, and we too find them as we wait patiently upon the Lord.

But as Christians our answers go beyond Habakkuk's. When we grieve for the suffering and tragedy about us, as we see the breakdown of morality and face the threat of the nuclear holocaust—and, in all this, as God seems silent—we can look back to Calvary. There, on Golgotha, God the Son has identified Himself with the misery, despair, and dereliction of the human lot.

During those hours on the cross, He remained silent, except for seven brief utterances. And today, in His silence, we know He is *there*—grieving, identifying with the pain of people.

Yes, believers raise the same questions as unbelievers. But because, like Paul, they know in whom they have believed, they find confidence—confidence in Christ, blessed assurance.

A Tale of Two Cities

[Hab. 2:5-20]

In the Bible two cities stand out.

One was never large in size. It struggled to survive through centuries of marauders' raids. Though devastated several times, it has risen, phoenixlike, from the dead again and again. After more than three millennia it still stands— although, as often in the past, it today faces threats from hostile neighbors.

The Bible has much to say about this city and its inhabitants. And in the prophetic scenario portraying the restoration of all things when sin and sinners are no more, the name of this city is perpetuated in the capital of the earth made new.

That city is Jerusalem.

The second city also had a long and checkered history. Its name appears in the Biblical record before Jerusalem finds mention. According to the ancient lists of the book of Genesis, this city was part of the kingdom founded by Nimrod, the great-grandson of Noah (Gen. 10:8-10). At first one of several city-states that grew up in the valleys of the Tigris and Euphrates, it eventually became the capital of an empire. By the time of the great king Hammurabi, famous for his code of law promulgated several centuries before Moses, the empire included all of Mesopotamia and expanded into Syria.

But the fortunes of the empire waned, and with them the prosperity of the city. The Hittites, Egyptians, and Assyrians became the dominant powers. However, after about one thousand years of obscurity the city revived. Under

Nabopolassar (626-605 B.C.) the ancient empire flourished again, setting the stage for the reign of his son, Nebuchadnezzar, under whose rule the city attained its golden age.

The city today lies in ruins. It is of interest only to the antiquarian and archeologist. But its name lives on in the Biblical text, for it stands as the rival of Jerusalem, both literal and spiritual. As Jerusalem in a spiritual sense represents God's system of truth, so spiritually this city denotes false religion and those systems of human devising by which men and women and governments seek to order their lives.

The city is Babylon.

Studying the book of Habakkuk, we encounter Babylon just as it began to rise to the zenith of its power. Although when Habakkuk actually wrote, the city's rise to renewed dominance was still a generation away, his prediction that the Chaldeans would overrun Palestine pointed to the invasions of Nebuchadnezzar. And Nebuchadnezzar, son of Nabopolassar, was the supreme ruler of the neo-Babylonian empire.

Habakkuk 2:5-20 lays out in unvarnished frankness the besetting sins of Nebuchadnezzar's Babylon. Pride, a false sense of security, injustice and violence, drunkenness and exploitation, idolatry—on these Babylonia built, and because of them she would fall under God's judgments.

In order to grasp why Habakkuk was so horrified to hear of God's plan to use the Babylonians as His agents of chastisement on Judah and Jerusalem, we have to get a picture of Nebuchadnezzar's Babylon. We have to see how this city, his pride and joy, dominated the minds of the people of his time and how elaborate was its system of idolatrous religion. Notice what archeology reveals.

Ancient Babylon

"Although ancient Babylon did not have the fantastic size attributed to it by Herodotus, the city was nevertheless of formidable size at a time when cities were very small according to modern standards. Its circumference of about

10 miles (16.09 kilometers) was comparable with the 7.5-mile (12.09 kilometer) circumference of Nineveh, the capital of Assyria's empire; with the walls of imperial Rome, 6 miles (9.6 kilometers) in circumference; and with the 4 miles (6.4 kilometers) of the walls of Athens at the time of that city's height in the fifth century B.C. This comparison with other famous cities of antiquity shows that Babylon was, with the possible exception of Egyptian Thebes, then in ruins, the largest and greatest of all ancient capitals, though it was much smaller than classical writers later pictured it. It is understandable why Nebuchadnezzar felt he had a right to boast of having built 'this great Babylon . . . by the might of my power" (Dan. 4:30).

"A City of Temples and Palaces.—Because Babylon contained the sanctuary of the god Marduk, considered to be the lord of heaven and earth, the chief of all the gods, the ancient Babylonians considered their city the 'navel' of the world. Hence, Babylon was a religious center without rival on earth. A cuneiform tablet of Nebuchadnezzar's time lists fifty-three temples dedicated to important gods, 955 small sanctuaries, and 384 street altars—all of them within the city confines. In comparison, Asshur, one of the chief cities of Assyria, with its thirty-four temples and chapels, made a comparatively poor impression. One can well understand why the Babylonians were proud of their city, saying, 'Babylon is the origin and center of all lands.' Their pride is reflected in Nebuchadnezzar's famous words quoted in the comment on chap. 4:30, and also in an ancient song of praise (as given by E. Ebeling, *Keilschrifttexte aus Assur religiösen Inhalts*, Part I [Leipzig, 1915], No. 8):

'O Babylon, whosoever beholds thee is
    filled with rejoicing,
Whosoever dwells in Babylon increases
    his life,
Whosoever speaks evil of Babylon is like
    one who kills his own mother.
Babylon is like a sweet date palm, whose
    fruit is lovely to behold.'

"The center of Babylon's glory was the famous temple tower *Etemenanki*, 'the foundation stone of heaven and earth,' 299 feet (91.1 meters) square at the base and probably more than 300 feet (91.4 meters) high. This edifice was surpassed in height in ancient times only by the two great pyramids at Giza in Egypt. The tower may have been built at the site where the Tower of Babel once stood. The brick structure consisted of seven stages, of which the smallest and uppermost was a shrine dedicated to Marduk, the chief god of Babylon. . . .

"A great temple complex, called *Esagila*, literally, 'He who raises the head,' surrounded the tower *Etemenanki*. Its courts and buildings were the scenes of many religious ceremonies performed in honor of Marduk. Great and colorful processions terminated at this place. With the exception of the great Amen temple at Karnak, *Esagila* was the largest and most famous of all temples of the ancient Orient. At the time Nebuchadnezzar ascended the throne it had already enjoyed a long and glorious history, and the new king entirely rebuilt and beautified extensive sections of the temple complex, incuding the tower *Etemenanki*.

"In both number and size the palaces of Babylon revealed extraordinary luxury. During his long reign of forty-three years Nebuchadnezzar built three large castles or palaces. One of them lay within the Inner City, the others outside it. One was what is known as the Summer Palace, in the northernmost part of the new eastern quarter. The mound that now covers its remains is the highest of those comprising the ruins of old Babylon, and is the only place that still bears the ancient name *Babil*. However, the thorough destruction of this palace in ancient times and the subsequent looting of the bricks of the structure have not left much for the archeologist to discover. Thus we know little regarding this palace.

"Another large palace, which excavators now call the Central Palace, lay immediately outside the northern wall of the Inner City. This, too, was built by Nebuchadnezzar. Modern archeologists found this large building also in a hopelessly desolate condition, with the exception of one part of the palace, the Museum of Antiquities. Here valuable objects of the glorious past of Babylonia's history, such as old statues, inscriptions, and trophies of war, had been collected and exhibited 'for men to behold,' as Nebuchadnezzar expressed it in one of his inscriptions.

"The Southern Palace lay in the northwestern corner of the Inner City and contained, among other structures, the famous hanging gardens, one of the Seven Wonders of the ancient world. A large vaulted building was surmounted with a roof garden irrigated by a system of pipes through which water was pumped up. According to Diodorus, Nebuchadnezzar built this marvelous edifice for his Median wife in order to give to her, in the midst of level and treeless Babylonia, a substitute for the wooded hills of her native land, which she missed. In the vaults underneath the roof gardens provisions of grain, oil, fruit, and spices were stored for the needs of the court and court dependents. Excavators found administrative documents in these rooms, some of which mention King Jehoiachin of Judah as the recipient of royal rations.

"Adjoining the hanging gardens was an extensive complex of buildings, halls, and rooms that had replaced the smaller palace of Nabopolassar, the father of Nebuchadnezzar. This Southern Palace was more or less the official residence of the king, the place where all ceremonies of state took place. In the center was a large throne room, 56 by 171 feet [17 by 52 meters], and possibly 60 feet [18 meters] high. This immense hall was probably the place where Belshazzar banqueted during the last night of his life, because no other hall in the palace was large enough to accommodate a thousand guests (see Dan. 5:1).

"One of that city's colorful structures was the famous Ishtar Gate which adjoined the Southern Palace and formed one of the northern entrances to the Inner City. This was the most beautiful of all Babylonian gates, for through it passed the Procession Street, leading from the various royal palaces to the temple *Esagila*. Fortunately, this gate was less completely destroyed than any other structure in Babylon and is now the most impressive of all extant ruins of the city. It still rises to a height of about 40 feet (12 meters).

"The interior structures of the city walls and gates, the palaces and temples, were of unbaked bricks. The outer coats consisted of baked and, in some instances, of glazed bricks. The outer bricks of the city walls were yellow in color, those of the gates sky blue, those of the palaces rose, and those of the temples white. The Ishtar Gate was a double structure, because of the double walls. It was 170 feet [50 meters] long and consisted of four towerlike structures of varying thickness and height. The walls were of bricks whose glazed surfaces formed raised figures of animals. There were at least 575 of these. There were bulls in yellow, with decorative rows of blue hair, and green hoofs and horns. These alternated with mythological beasts in yellow, called *sirrush*, which had serpents' heads and tails, scaled bodies, and eagles' and cats' feet. . . .

"The approach to the Ishtar Gate . . . was lined on both sides of the street with defensive walls. On these walls were glazed-brick lions in relief, either white with yellow manes or yellow with red manes (now turned green) on a blue background.

"Such was this colorful and mighty city that King Nebuchadnezzar had built—the marvel of all nations. His pride in it is reflected in inscriptions he left to posterity. One of them, now in the Berlin Museum, reads as follows:

" 'I have made Babylon, the holy city, the glory of the great gods, more prominent than before, and have promoted its rebuilding. I have caused the sanctuaries of gods and goddesses to lighten up like the day. No king among all kings has ever created, no earlier king has ever built, what I have magnificently built for Marduk. I have furthered to the utmost the equipment of *Esagila*, and the renovation of Babylon more than had ever been done before. All my valuable works, the beautification of the sanctuaries of the great gods, which I undertook more than my royal ancestors, I wrote in a document and put it down for coming generations. All my deeds, which I have written in this document, shall those read who know [how to read] and remember the glory of the great gods. May the way of my life be long, may I rejoice in offspring; may my offspring rule over the blackheaded people into all eternity, and may the mentioning of my name be proclaimed for good at all future times.' "—*The SDA Bible Commentary*, vol. 4, pp. 797-799.

Babylon Today

Although Nebuchadnezzar's Babylon, "the glory of kingdoms, the splendor and pride of the Chaldeans" (Isa. 13:19), today lies desolate, spiritual Babylon lives on. Her pride in human attainments and confusion of religious ideas still captivate the minds of men and women everywhere.

In this end-time generation God announces the doom of spiritual Babylon: "Fallen, fallen is Babylon the great, she who made all nations drink the wine of her impure passion" (Rev. 14:8). Babylon has "become a dwelling place of demons, a haunt of every foul spirit, a haunt of every foul and hateful bird" (Rev. 18:2). So His call to the world is "Come out of her, my people, lest you take part in her sins, lest you share in her plagues; for her sins are heaped high as heaven, and God has remembered her iniquities" (Rev. 18:4, 5).

Look at spiritual Babylon. No need to take a jet plane to the Middle East. Babylon is next door—maybe right inside your house. Babylon lurks all around us—and it is rich and attractive and powerful. But Babylon is still Babylon, the Babylon summoned to judgment by the God of Habakkuk.

1. *Pride:* A century ago the German philosopher Nietzsche published *Thus Spake Zarathustra*, in which he set out the thesis: "God is dead. . . . But I give you superman." That thesis characterizes twentieth-century man.

Gerhard Niemyer, of Notre Dame University, has characterized modern man in an article "The 'Autonomous' Man." He is "(1) man without a father, having divested himself not merely of his heavenly Father, but also of his earthly parents, his forebears, and the past in general; (2) man without a

Creator, who . . . refuses to acknowledge any dependence of his on anyone or anything; particularly for his life; (3) man without any judge, either in heaven or on earth, who deems himself unaccountable either to his fellowmen or to a divine judge."

But God is not mocked. Men and women may choose to ignore Him, they may follow their own devices in the pride of their hearts, but God is still *there*. Because He exists and is the moral arbiter of the universe, He "will bring every deed into judgment, with every secret thing, whether good or evil" (Eccl. 12:14).

2. *False security:* The world outlay on arms has reached an incredible figure. Not only the United States and the U.S.S.R. are involved. Even poor and small nations that are struggling to provide sufficient food for their people are hungry for weapons.

Once nations fought each other with swords and bows and arrows. They built strong walls around their cities and massive gates that could be locked shut to keep out the invader. But then came the battering ram, and after that gunpowder, and finally rockets and atomic weapons. The invention of the airplane made obsolete the last defense offered by the city. And the weapons continue to proliferate, both in numbers and advancing technology—from ABMs and MIRVs we have come to the MX and the Star Wars system.

The quest for security—for the ultimate place of safety—has proved to be elusive. Despite the enormous sums spent on defense, the life of every person on Planet Earth today hangs under the Damoclean sword of nuclear annihilation.

Where can we find security? Not in any new weapon, not in any confederation of the nations, not in human hopes. Only in God: "The Lord is good, a stronghold in the day of trouble; he knows those who take refuge in him" (Nahum 1:7).

3. *Injustice and violence:* For all our learning, the late twentieth century at times seems very much like the jungle.

Consider:

● Some of the wealthiest people pay little tax or no tax at all. The IRS estimates that $90 *billion* does not find its way into the treasury each year.

● Victims of crime are concentrated among the poor and the aged. The affluent buy deadbolt locks and burglar alarms and guard dogs to protect themselves.

● Integrity is a scarce commodity. "In the past, breaking the rules was viewed as an exception. Now such behavior is considered commonplace," notes Jerald Jellison, professor of psychology at the University of Southern California. He cites tax evasion, shoplifting, falsification of résumés, selling of term papers and reports, graft in government, cheating by welfare recipients, marital infidelity, and crooked business deals.

4. *Alcohol:* According to the Center for Science in the Public Interest, approximately 15 million Americans have serious alcohol problems. An estimated 3 million of these are juveniles.

Alcohol kills more than 100,000 people each year in the United States alone. It costs the nation $120 billion through personal and property damage, hospitalization costs, industrial losses, and imprisonment.

The manufacturers of alcoholic beverages in the United States spend about $750 million in advertising on TV and radio alone. Estimates for 1986 project a figure of about $1 billion.

Since television became popular in the fifties, per capita consumption of alcohol has increased more than 40 percent. Between 1962 and 1982 consumption of alcoholic beverages increased as a percentage of all beverages—from 17.3 gallons per person to 28.4 gallons. Milk, on the other hand, decreased from 33 gallons per person to 27 gallons during the same period of time.

Alcohol is a massive evil. The Christian should have nothing to do with it and instead should unite to reduce its power over the lives of millions.

With both literal and spiritual Babylon, wine—literal and

spiritual—is the means of enslaving and shaming humanity. And it falls under God's judgment.

5. *Idols:* The book of Isaiah in particular casts scorn on the worship of idols. In a mocking passage the prophet pictures the huge idols of Babylon, powerless to save the city and themselves borne away by beasts struggling under the burden of their weight. "Bel bows down, Nebo stoops, their idols are on beasts and cattle; these things you carry are loaded as burdens on weary beasts. They stoop, they bow down together, they cannot save the burden, but themselves go into captivity" (Isa. 46:1, 2).

Most modern people in the West will consider idolatry incredibly stupid. But let us not pass judgment so quickly. We also fall prey to modern idolatry. Anything that we value more than God, anything or anyone that commands our first loyalty—that is an idol. So the idol could be our work, our home, our sports, our spouse, our own selves.

All idols, in the final analysis, cannot help us in the hour of direst need. No matter what confidence we may place in any human institution, program, invention, activity, it is not fail-safe. Only God does not fail, and that is why He refuses to share His glory with any other.

A tale of two cities—Jerusalem and Babylon. One symbolizes the vast network of human devisings; one the city of God. One comes under judgment; the other becomes the capital of the new earth, where God wipes away every tear and the gates are never shut.

Formula for Revival

[Hab. 3:1-19]

The third chapter of Habakkuk, little noticed in these days, holds tremendous importance for God's people. The key word of the chapter is *revival*, or *renewal*. The chapter shows us the way to revival: revival as the church's greatest need, the promise of revival, and how revival comes.

Revival—the Church's Greatest Need

The prophet prays for the renewal of his people: "O Lord, I have heard thy speech, and was afraid: O Lord, revive thy work in the midst of the years, in the midst of the years make known; in wrath remember mercy" (Hab. 3:2, K.J.V.). In the R.S.V. these words are translated as: "O Lord, I have heard the report of thee, and thy work, O Lord, do I fear. In the midst of the years renew it; in the midst of the years make it known; in wrath remember mercy."

What a change from the spirit of the first chapter of the book! Instead of doubts and questions, we hear how the prophet has worked through his problems. Now he realizes that the greatest need for his people is that God will bring revival, renewal.

Throughout the Scriptures holy men of God call His people to a renewing of their religious experience. Some of these pleas come during times of deep apostasy or of distress and tribulation; others do not arise from a particular situation of need. But the fact is that God's people *always* stand in need of revival. So long as we are in the world, the world will rain its fallout upon us. We must constantly be turning back to God, finding our life and strength in Him.

In the Old Testament two books apart from Habakkuk especially stand out because of their calls for revival.

The first is the book of Hosea, addressed to the northern kingdom of Israel. The ten tribes, drifting ever further into apostasy and Baal worship, faced the sure threat of destruction and loss of their nation. But they paid no heed to their danger or to their spiritual state. Hosea pleaded with them to turn back to the Lord. He longed that they should come to experience renewal. "I will return again to my place, until they acknowledge their guilt and seek my face, and in their distress they seek me, saying, 'Come, let us return unto the Lord; for he has torn, that he may heal us; he has stricken, and he will bind us up. After two days will he revive us; on the third day he will raise us up, that we may live before him. Let us know, let us press on to know the Lord; his going forth is sure as the dawn; he will come to us as the showers, as the spring rains that water the earth' " (chap 5:15-6:3).

The prophet's appeal was: "Return, O Israel, to the Lord your God, for you have stumbled because of your iniquity. Take with you words and return to the Lord; say to him, 'Take away all iniquity; accept that which is good and we will render the fruit of our lips. Assyria shall not save us, we will not ride upon horses; and we will not say any more, "Our God," to the work of our hands. In thee the orphan finds mercy' " (Hosea 14:1-3).

The book of Joel, a work of only three chapters, also contains a powerful call for revival. This book apparently was written at a time of natural disaster. The land, once flowing with milk and honey, had been blasted by locust plagues, drought, and fire. The prophet sees that even greater disasters lie ahead, as invading armies are about to devastate the land.

Yet all hope was not gone. If God's people would return to Him in sincerity, the threat of further destruction might be forestalled. " 'Yet even now,' says the Lord, 'return to me with all your heart, with fasting, with weeping, and with mourning: and rend your hearts and not your garments.' Return unto the Lord, your God, for he is gracious and merciful, slow to anger, and abounding in steadfast love, and repents of evil. Who knows whether he will not turn and repent, and leave a blessing behind him, a cereal offering and a drink offering for the Lord, your God?" (Joel 2:12-14).

The work of revival for which Joel called was to be nationwide in scope. It was to encompass the elders, the lay people, even the children. "Blow the trumpet in Zion; sanctify a fast; call a solemn assembly; gather the people. Sanctify the congregation; assemble the elders; gather the children, even nursing infants. Let the bridegroom leave his room, and the bride her chamber" (verses 15, 16).

Revival is still the greatest need of God's people. As Seventh-day Adventists, we can look back on a marvelous past and on a work that is going from strength to strength worldwide. As we think of what God has done and continues to do for us, we exclaim, " 'What has God wrought!' " (Num. 23:23). But despite the growth of the church, despite the fine institutions we have and the programs that have proved themselves over and over, revival is still our greatest need. Our strength comes not in buildings, not in programs, not in statistics of growth— although we rejoice in them—but in the Lord. The church will reach greatness only as it stays in tune with the Master.

One of the most outstanding appeals made by Ellen G. White for revival and reformation was published in the *Review and Herald* of March 22, 1887, under the title "The Church's Great Need." She said: "A revival of true godliness among us is the greatest and most urgent of all our needs. To seek this should be our first work. There must be earnest effort to obtain the blessing of the Lord, not because God is not willing to bestow His blessing upon us, but because we are unprepared to receive it." And in the February 25, 1902, *Review* she said, "A revival and a reformation must take place, under the ministration of the Holy Spirit."

We need a renewal of spiritual life. We need to seek after God, to hunger and thirst for His righteousness. We need to get back to daily study of His Word, to the quiet hour with Him early every morning.

No one else can eat for us. No one else can drink for us. We go into the kingdom one by one. We cannot look to our pastors, our teachers, our parents, or our friends for spiritual life. They may help and nurture us, but each of us must come into touch with the living God.

Those of us who are heavily involved in the work of the Lord need to safeguard our individual spiritual experience. We may be employed by the church, but let us beware of thinking that the very environment in which we labor or the work in which we are engaged will somehow safeguard our relationship to the Lord. Our only protection is in daily turning to the Lord and away from the world, seeking His will, feeding upon the Scriptures.

This fact was brought home to me in dramatic fashion some years ago when I was a student at Andrews University. I had come to the seminary as an older student, one already ordained and on furlough after nearly six years of service in India. I was enjoying the classes, the resources of the James White Library, the chapel services, and the fellowship with faculty and students. But one day, as a group of students were talking, I heard a young man blurt out, "You won't find God in this place!"

What had happened? The young man had come to Andrews University with a clear sense of God's leading. But apparently he felt that somehow the environment—the teachers, the students, the books, the classes, the spiritual activities—would take care of his spiritual needs. He forgot to keep up that spiritual life, to renew it day by day. The result? He lost what he had when he came to the seminary.

We also need a renewal of practical Christianity. "The world is too much with us," as the poet Wordsworth observed; "late and soon, getting and spending, we lay waste our powers." We have spent our energies on things that are not bread, on drink that does not satisfy. We Seventh-day Adventists have a banquet of spiritual food—and the world around us is starving!

We live in an incredibly selfish age. Even in spiritual things we can become selfish. We can spend a lot of time congratulating ourselves, like the Pharisee who thanked God that he was not like other people!

A friend of mine, a young pastor involved in youth work, told of an experience that brought home this realization to him. He had made the acquaintance of two young people from the counterculture—Debbie and Dan, who had very low self-esteem. The pastor took them along to a study group where Adventist youth were exploring various Biblical themes.

Debbie and Dan sat silently as they heard the members of the group talking about the new life in Christ. They hardly knew the Scriptures, and they sat quietly as the group fell into an argument. Some of the young people held the position that because we have a healthy self-esteem we have the confidence to come to Jesus, while the rest took just the opposite view—after we come to Jesus we acquire a healthy self-image.

The pastor was so involved in the discussion that he forgot all about Debbie and Dan. With a start he turned to look at them. There was Debbie, her face shining with the ideas that she was hearing. And there was Dan, tears running down his face and onto his beard. A miracle was taking place, as Debbie and Dan were finding the new life in Jesus. But the Adventist young people were so involved in the argument that they couldn't see the miracle.

We need a renewal of love.

Recently I was visiting in a foreign field and sat down at the home of a minister. There we were around the table—husband, wife, and two sons. During the course of the conversation I asked the group what they thought was the greatest need of the church in that field. Immediately the older son, who is studying to be a lawyer, shot back, "Our greatest need here is love."

I think that is true worldwide. Too often we are more concerned to be right in our ideas regardless of the spirit in which we hold or present those ideas. We need less of the spirit of condemnation and more of the spirit of acceptance.

Some of the sharpest things Ellen White wrote she addressed to Uriah Smith. In the years following the controversy of righteousness by faith that erupted at the Minneapolis General Conference in 1888, Uriah Smith had much growing to do. Ellen White told him that she would have nothing to do with his ideas so long as they were accompanied by the negative spirit he was cherishing. For her, the spirit of the ideas made it clear that they could not be from God. Fortunately, Uriah Smith eventually harkened to her admonitions and strong rebukes.

We today need a renewal of our identity and mission.

We need to wake up to the flight of the years, to realize that we are looking for Jesus to return. We need to proclaim Him in boldness and love—our Saviour, Lord of the Sabbath, heavenly high priest and judge, and coming king.

God's people need to wake up—to who they are, to what they are, to why they are in this world. Time is short, and the Lord is coming! There is a heaven to win and a hell to shun. There is a world to be informed, millions upon millions who have not yet heard the good news of Jesus.

Revival, renewal—surely here is the church's greatest need!

The Promise of Revival

Our God is the God of new life. He promises, " 'Behold, I make all things new' " (Rev. 21:5). He is the one who, as Paul said, is able to bring life to the dead, to bring into being things that are not (Rom. 4:17).

Every year God shows His power to bring new life by the miracle of the spring. How often have I looked out on a January landscape, mute and crystalline with ice and snow. The wind cuts like a whetted knife, gathering up snowflakes and hurling them against trunks of oaks and maples, gaunt and gray against the northern sky. As I have looked at this scene I have wondered, Does anything stir beneath the snow? Can this ocean of windswept white bring forth the honeysuckle and the rose?

Yes, January's howling blast will become heavy with April's showers, and the buried flowers will find a dream. God's recurring miracle of life from the dead earth is a promise to us in our spiritual life. He is able to revive us individually; He is able to revive the church collectively.

Hope—that is the message that comes from the Scriptures. We are saved by hope, says Paul (chap. 8:24). Hope is one member of his famous trilogy (1 Cor. 13:13).

Habakkuk also found this truth. Although his dialogue with God began in perplexity, frustration, and doubt, his book ends with confident assurance. The third chapter, a hymn composed by Habakkuk himself and prepared for string accompaniment, recalls God's mighty deeds on behalf of His people. It overflows with allusions from Israel's history—from the crossing of the Red Sea, from battles with enemies, from the giving of the law at Mount Sinai. Its message is this: The God who acted to bring salvation in days of old is just the same today. Habakkuk, recall what God has done and take heart!

Yes, revival *is* our greatest need. The church is frail, weak, and defective. As we review our experiences, we have to confess that we have done what we should not have done and have left undone the things that we should. "We have not known Thee as we ought"—this must be our confession.

But in the Lord is our hope. Although the church is weak and often wandering, it still is the object of God's highest regard. In a revolted world, it is His fortress. The church is the repository of the riches of His grace. Individually and collectively we are accepted in the Beloved.

How, then, will the Lord come to us in revival? In just the same manner as He has come to us in the past.

Recall the time when you first met the Lord. Remember that day, perhaps many years ago, when you made a solemn promise to be His child. Recall the thrill of resolution, the joy that came from the knowledge of His salvation, the peace of the Spirit. This was the way the Lord first came to you and brought salvation.

And when He comes, bringing revival, it is the same Lord, and He will come in the same way. He can take our worn-out lives, our broken resolutions, our faded hopes, and make all things new. He can make us His little children once more—new in hope, new in fervor, new in determination, new in power.

Christianity is a transforming friendship. It is far more than doctrines and dogma; much more than rituals and rites; infinitely more than a set of rules and laws. It is knowing Jesus Christ as our Lord and Saviour, knowing Him personally, knowing Him as our friend.

But like any relationship, Christianity can run down—and become stale. A man and a woman who have been friends and lovers for years can find their relationship going stale. They may begin to take each other for granted. They may no longer pay attention to each other with little tokens of affection. The excitement, the zest, the elements of creativity and unpredictability that mark courtship may leak away as marriage becomes humdrum and boring.

Human relationships can be renewed, and so can the Christian's relationship with Jesus Christ. Because we worship the God who brings life from the dead, who brings into being things that are not, who promises to bring revival, there is hope. No matter how far we have fallen away from our first promises and first experience, there is hope.

How Revival Comes

1. *God is the source of any revival.* New life can come only from God. We may try as hard as we like to bring revival, but we cannot dictate it. It is the Spirit who gives life, and He is not at the dictation of men and women.

Habakkuk had to learn this lesson. His book starts out with a strong element of telling God what to do, almost rebuking Yahweh for His seeming inaction. Habakkuk was quite ready to tell the Lord what He should be about!

But after he had gone into his watchtower and waited for the Lord, his thinking changed. Habakkuk came to realize that God was very much in control, and although events around the prophet seemed to be chaotic, the Lord was still watching over His earth and His people. He had acted mightily in times past, and He would act again.

As we sigh and cry over the abominations done in the land and the seeming coldness of people in the church, let us not take upon ourselves what belongs to God. Let us supplicate Him. Let us beseech Him. And let us hope in Him in confident assurance, even as the prophet at last came to do.

2. *We must prepare the way for God to work.* Says Ellen White: "There must be earnest effort to obtain the blessing of the Lord, not because God is not willing to bestow His blessing upon us, but because we are unprepared to receive it. Our heavenly Father is more willing to give His Holy Spirit to them that ask Him, than are earthly parents to give good gifts to their children. But it is our work, by confession, humiliation, repentance, and earnest prayer, to fulfill the conditions upon which God has promised to grant us His blessing. A revival need be expected only in answer to prayer. . . . Let us confess and forsake every sin, that the way of the Lord may be prepared, that He may come into our assemblies and impart His rich grace. The world, the flesh, and the devil must be overcome."—*Selected Messages*, book 1, pp. 121-123.

We cannot manipulate or engineer revival, but we can frustrate it. We can stand in the way of God's purposes, cutting off the sweet action of His Spirit, who seeks to bring new life to the church.

3. *Preparation for revival is an individual work.* We should not hope to see the whole church revived. That time will never come. Revival comes to individuals. "There are persons in the church who are not converted, and who will not unite in earnest, prevailing prayer. We must enter upon the work individually. We must pray more, and talk less," says Ellen White *(ibid.,* p. 122).

Adventists have a peculiar temptation to put off to the future what God designs that we should enjoy today. We are people of expectation, expecting the time of the latter rain, expecting the finishing of the work, expecting the glad return of our Lord. With such thinking we easily can be caught in a trap—to believe that somehow the mass movement of the last days, when the Spirit of God is poured upon the church and thousands are converted in a day, will embrace us.

Such thinking is wrong on two counts.

First, it is dangerous. We have no assurance that we will still be around to enjoy the blessings of the latter rain and the close of the work. Even if we should be, we may not be ready to receive the "latter rain" unless we already have received the "early rain."

Second, God designs that individually we may have the latter-rain experience today. He is more willing to give than we are to receive. If we would open our hearts to Him, casting ourselves upon His goodness and grace, even today we might know the power of His new life.

Yes, revival is the church's greatest need. But the point is this: Revival is *my* greatest need! So, am I ready to pray Habakkuk's prayer and give it an individual slant, "O Lord, revive Thy work in the midst of the years" (chap. 3:2, N.A.S.B.)—that is, renew Thy work *in me* in the midst of the years? And am I prepared to help that prayer find its God-designed fulfillment by removing every obstacle that the Spirit may work?

In Absolute Confidence

Edmund Gosse, in a moving passage in his book *Father and Son*, describes the effect of his father's reading from the book of Hebrews to him when he was a boy: " 'The extraordinary beauty of the language—for instance, the matchless cadences and images of the first chapter—made a certain impression upon my imagination, and were (I think) my earliest initiation into the magic of literature. I was incapable of defining what I felt, but I certainly had a grip in the throat, which was in its essence a purely aesthetic emotion, when my father read, in his pure, large, ringing voice, such passages as "The heavens are the work of thy hands: They shall perish, but thou remainest; and they shall all wax old as doth a garment; and as a vesture shalt thou fold them up, and they shall be changed: but thou art the same, and thy years shall not fail." But the dialectic parts of the epistle puzzled and confused me. Such metaphysical ideas as "laying again the foundation of repentance from dead works" and "crucifying . . . the Son of God afresh" were not successfully brought down to the level of my understanding. . . . The melodious language, the divine forensic audacities, the magnificent ebb and flow of argument which make the Epistle to the Hebrews such a miracle, were far beyond my reach, and they only bewildered me.' "—Quoted in James Moffatt, *A Critical and Exegetical Commentary on the Epistle to the Hebrews* (Edinburgh: T. & T. Clark, 1924).

Gosse's view of Hebrews is by no means uncommon. Even for many adult Christians the book remains an enigma—admired for its magnificent language and theological profundity, but obscure nonetheless. Adventists, who have grown up learning that Hebrews is important for the faith, may find it too heavy for frequent study.

Some years ago Hebrews provided the topic for a quarter's Sabbath school lessons. I was interested to observe the reaction of teachers and students to the material. Week by week I heard complaints that class members either weren't understanding the book or else didn't see how the lessons applied to their lives today. At last we came to Hebrews 11, and the teacher said as he began the class, "Well, *finally* we've reached a passage we can understand!"

This neglect of Hebrews is a great theological and spiritual loss. Over the years I have spent more time with this book than any other of the Scriptures and have found it enlightening and enriching. Every time I return to Hebrews for further study I am amazed at the new insights it provides. To me, Hebrews is an inexhaustible mine of divine truth.

Granted, Hebrews isn't easy reading (but was Scripture intended to be so?), but neither is it as difficult as many people imagine. And as we begin to grasp its meaning we are amazed at how directly it speaks to Christian life today.

In this chapter I will list seven points that I have found helpful for the study of Hebrews. Finally I will briefly compare and contrast Hebrews with Habakkuk.

How to Understand Hebrews

1. *The chief concern of Hebrews is practical.*

That may come as a surprise. Many Christians think of Hebrews as a theological treatise, but it isn't. Although it contains profound theological reasoning, the apostle himself calls it a "word of exhortation" (Heb. 13:22).

Even the title is misleading in the King James Version: "The Epistle of Paul the Apostle to the Hebrews." The oldest manuscripts simply have "To the Hebrews." In several respects Hebrews doesn't follow the pattern of the New Testament letters. We find no identification of the author, no mention of the recipients, no word of greeting. Instead,

the document plunges headlong into a theological statement: "In many and various ways God spoke . . ." Nor does
the writing show that spontaneous, itemized character—
taking up topics, problems, or questions in turn—that we
expect in a letter. Instead it follows the form of a measured
argument that rolls on in calculated, steady flow.

In fact, Hebrews is not really a letter. It is best described
as a written sermon. Unlike a letter, which may arise out of
deep emotion and be written at feverish pace (as was
Galatians, for instance), a sermon results from careful
planning, yet is not written in isolation from life. It
continually has in mind the hearers and their needs. So in
the sermon to the Hebrews the theological reasoning, for all
its complexity, serves a specific, practical end in the lives of
its original recipients.

The Hebrews were Christians of long standing. But
therein lies a danger: Our religion can become tired, the vital
force can gradually ebb away. That was the problem facing
the early believers addressed in the apostle's sermon.

In chapter 2:1-4 the apostle's counsel focuses in the
words *drift* or *slip* of verse 1 and *neglect* of verse 3. The first
term is an interesting one in the Greek. The apostle chooses
a nautical metaphor used for flowing by, slipping away,
being washed away, drifting away. As night winds and
currents may carry a ship, apparently safe at anchor, out of
the harbor, so Christians have to beware lest they drift from
the harbor of salvation. The word can apply also to a ring
that slips off the finger and is lost (hence the K.J.V. "slip").
The idea is similiar—the possibility of a gradual loss
occurring unbeknown.

The second term, translated "neglect," signifies "disregard," "lack of concern." We note that it is *"so great
salvation"* (K.J.V.) or, as *The New English Bible* has it,
"deliverance so great," that is at stake. The apostle is not
here warning against a deliberate rejection of Christianity.
Instead, he worries about the possibility of its neglect. It is
because Christianity is so *precious* that we must not take it
for granted. The value of the religion calls for a zeal that

acknowledges its worth. When salvation is so great, how can the one who treats it casually escape divine retribution?

We find a second series of exhortations in chapters 3:1-4:13. Here the word *harden* surfaces. The idea is similar to what we found in chapter 2:1-4, although the metaphor has changed—that of the gradual loss of spiritual powers. It is the "heart" that hardens by the relentless inroads of the *apatē* (deceitfulness or pleasures) of sin. Such a heart—an evil, unfaithful heart—may lead at length to a falling away (literally, "apostasy"), a dropping out from the community, just as the children of Israel wandered away from devotion to the Lord and perished in the desert (chap. 3:7-15).

The apostle's counsel now takes on a new dimension. While he speaks of the hardening—the slow, insidious corrupting of the heart—he adds the ideas of disobedience and rebellion (verses 16-10; chap. 4:6, 11). Here we see a decline of religious experience that goes beyond mere neglect. In fact, the author raises the grim possibility that the subtle power of sin may even pervert the heart until it overtly defies its Lord.

A third section of the sermon, chapters 5:11-6:20, sheds much light on the nature of the community and its spiritual dangers. The apostle now rebukes his hearers because of their lack of growth. They ought to be teachers, but instead need to learn the ABCs of God's oracles. Rather than developing to maturity, they are spiritual infants. They have become "dull of hearing" (chap. 5:11-14).

The illustration from agriculture (chap. 6:7-12) drives the thought home. Land that receives bountiful rain must produce its harvest; otherwise it is accursed. Likewise, Christians should bear evidence of the blessings of God in their lives or they will lose them. The problem addressed resembles the one we have seen in the earlier exhortations against neglect and hardening of the heart. Here the author admonishes the readers, lest they become lazy or sluggish instead of maintaining a persevering faith to the end (verses 11, 12).

At the same time we see a vivid picture of the possibility

of open rejection of the values of the community. The warning in chapter 6:4-6 is one of the most startling of the entire Bible and has evoked intense study by Christians from the earliest times. For now we need simply note the three key words in the portrayal of denial of Jesus: falling away (literally, *apostasy*, as in chap. 3:12), "crucifying the Son of God" again (N.E.B.) (or, crucifying "on their own account" [R.S.V.], or with their own hands), and exposing Him to contempt (or "making mock of his death" [N.E.B.]). It is a sad, grim picture. Could it be possible that someone blessed of the Spirit and nurtured on the Word of God could one day come to the point of open, public repudiation of Christ and His cross? Yes, says the apostle. Yes, even this. So be careful!

A fourth passage, chapter 10:19-39, embodies the twofold dangers of neglect and rejection that we have noticed already. We find here, on the one hand, the peril of wavering, of neglecting the public assembly of the people of God, of forgetting the "former days" of Christian steadfastness, of casting away confidence in the certainty of the triumph of God's program, and of shrinking back (verses 23-25, 32-39). But we find also a passage strikingly reminiscent of chapter 6:4-6. Here the Christian sins willfully (deliberately, with a high hand), spurning the Son of God, profaning the blood of the covenant, and outraging the Spirit (chap. 10:26-31).

The apostle returns to exhortation in the final two chapters of his sermon. His advice shows that his hearers face the danger of growing weary, of gradually dropping out under the hardships of Christian life. They may neglect to show hospitality or to remember their fellows, or they may fall into idolatry, immorality, the love of money, or the snare of false teachings (chaps. 12:3-14; 13:1-9). At the same time he introduces the example of Esau (chap. 12:15-17). He was *bebēlos*, that is, profane, godless, irreligious. Because of his disregard for spiritual privileges he eventually lost the blessing of the birthright and found no way to recover it. In the same way the peril of rejection and refusal always remains a fearsome possibility for the Christians. So "see that you do not refuse him who is speaking" (verse 25).

These passages have given us a fairly clear spiritual profile of the recipients of Hebrews. Their problem is not false teachers who have swept their young feet off the ground, as in Galatia. Nor is it a heady enthusiasm because of manifestations of the Spirit, as in Corinth. It is not the question of the failure of the Jews to receive the gospel, as in Romans. No, their problem is one of *tired blood.* They have grown weary with waiting for the Lord's return, sluggish in their Christian identity. They question the value of their religion, more so as hard times for Christians loom on the horizon.

Spiritual weariness is dangerous: This is the apostle's message. Over and over, as we have seen, he hammers home its fearful results. Either, he suggests, we grow neglectful of our privileges, taking lightly what is of supreme value, or we may turn in defiant rejection of the entire Christian faith, taking our place among the majority who do not confess Jesus as Saviour and Lord. One end is as dire as the other.

2. *Hebrews should be studied as a whole.*

Too often people try to jump into the river of Hebrews halfway along its course. They get involved in arguing about disputed verses in chapters 9 or 10, for instance, instead of starting at the beginning of the book. Hebrews is like a mighty river winding its way to the sea. Along the course of its progress, every turn, every waterfall, has been carefully charted from the beginning. We understand the book and do justice to its reasoning only as we start where the author starts and let him disclose his logic to us.

In fact, the opening words of Hebrews set the course for the rest of the book. The first four verses are far more than an introduction, a way of getting our feet wet, as it were. These verses—one continuous sentence in Greek—set out the themes that the author develops in the later chapters. (In chapter 5 of this book we shall look at these four verses in detail.)

My conviction is this: Hebrews discloses its meaning to the careful reader if we will allow the book to speak for itself.

3. *Hebrews is constructed according to a regular pattern.*

When we look closely at the document, we begin to notice an *alternation* of theology and exhortation. We readily recognize the latter by the change from the third person to the first or second person plural, usually with the hortatory "Let us . . ." and often with the conjunction "therefore." For instance, all the first chapter involves theological discourse, but as soon as we come to chapter 2, we notice, "Therefore we must pay the closer attention . . ."

The first four verses of chapter 2 divert from theology (or better, *apply* the theology) in exhortation. In verse 5 the apostle reverts to the third person and has clearly moved back on the theological track.

Thus, the following laminated pattern of Hebrews emerges:

Theology	1:1-14
Exhortation	2:1-4
Theology	2:5-3:6a
Exhortation	3:6b-4:16
Theology	5:1-10
Exhortation	5:11-6:20
Theology	7:11-10:18
Exhortation	10:19-13:25

This pattern is unique in the New Testament. While all writings of the New Testament involve practical matters, none has the regular pattern displayed by Hebrews.

An awareness of this pattern aids the careful student of Hebrews. For instance, already in describing the spiritual profile of the Hebrews we had, in fact, raked through the exhortations of the sermon. Likewise, in tracing the theological development of the book, we can concentrate on those portions that we have identified as theology.

4. *Hebrews systematically presents theological argument.*

The apostle introduces each idea in the appropriate place, then develops and rounds it off. Each motif blends into the total argument to produce a composition of great logical force. Apart from its spiritual powers, the document is a masterpiece of ordered thinking. (And so we ought to note every word with great care—more so than in some more hurried works, where we look for the ideas.) For instance, notice the following ideas of Hebrews:

a. Purification: introduced at chapter 1:3, developed in chapters 9:1-10:18

b. High priest: introduced at chapter 2:17, 18, expanded at chapters 4:14-16 and 5:1-10, fully expounded at chapter 7:1-10:18.

c. Angels: introduced at chapter 1:4, developed in verses 5-14, wound up at chapter 2:16.

d. Covenant: introduced at chapter 7:22, developed in chapter 8:6-13, rounded off at chapters 9:18 and 10:16-18.

e. Faith: introduced at chapter 2:17, expanded in chapter 3:1-6, developed fully in chapter 11

5. *Hebrews carefully balances the old with the new.*

On the one hand, the apostle does not put down the Old Testament. Far from it. It is the record of the speaking of God. All those aspects of Israel's religion—the sanctuary, the sacrificial system, the Levitical and Aaronic priesthood—were given by the Lord Himself. Those students of Hebrews who have tended to denigrate the Old Testament and its system of religion need to remember this.

But on the other hand, the apostle draws a contrast. The New Testament is not merely a continuation of the Old. While the one God stands behind both, there is a qualitative distinction grounded in the supreme worth of the Son's person and deeds. Throughout the book of Hebrews we shall need to think clearly and maintain this balancing act if we would be true to its argument.

Thus, as we move from the Old to the New we find both continuity and discontinuity. The one God is behind both: This is the great common factor. But the one God has revealed Himself supremely in Jesus Christ the Son, whose death on Calvary is an all-sufficient sacrifice for the sins of mankind, whether committed during Old Testament times or later. Here is the element of discontinuity.

Hebrews maintains a careful balance between the Old

and the New. The apostle avoids collapsing the New into the Old, but he also avoids setting forth the New in such a manner as to make it totally apart from the Old. In following his trend of thought, we must be careful to strike the balance he has found under the inspiration of the Spirit.

6. *A key idea of Hebrews is the word* better.

Hebrews does not contrast the bad (Old) with the good (New). Rather, the contrast is between the good and the better.

The entire book may be outlined as follows:
The better revelation (chap. 1:1-4)
The better name (chaps. 1:5-2:18)
The better leader (chaps. 3:1-4:13)
The better priest (chaps. 4:14-6:20)
The better priesthood (chap. 7:1-28)
The better ministry (chap. 8:1-13)
The better sacrifice (chaps. 9:1-10:18)
The better country (chaps. 10:19-12:2)
The better city (chaps. 12:3-13:25)

To Christians grown weary in the way, Hebrews sets forth the magnificence of the person and work of Jesus. He is better than the angels, better than Moses, better than Aaron. He is high priest of a better sanctuary, mediator of a better covenant, provider of a better sacrifice for sins—one that truly deals with the age-old problem—and better example, who will take us through victoriously to the better country and better city.

7. *The central idea of the book of Hebrews is full assurance in Jesus Christ.*

Hebrews 10:19-23 best sums up the sermon: "Brothers, since the blood of Jesus assures our entrance into the sanctuary by the new and living path he has opened up for us through the veil (the 'veil' meaning his flesh), and since we have a great priest who is over the house of God, let us draw near in utter sincerity and absolute confidence, our hearts sprinkled clean from the evil which lay on our conscience and our bodies washed in pure water. Let us hold unswervingly to our profession which gives us hope, for he who made the promise deserves our trust" (N.A.B.).

In absolute confidence—this expression summarizes the message of Hebrews. It covers both the *what* and the *so what* of Christianity. The what, because (as we shall see in subsequent chapters) we have a superlative Lord. Jesus is both fully God and fully man, our sinless high priest who ever ministers the benefits of His sacrifice in the heavenly courts on our behalf. And the so what, because as Christians we can never be the same as we were before we met Jesus. The cleansing provided in His blood transforms us. Christianity involves friendship with the living Lord, the joyful experience of walking with Him day by day. In walking with Him, we are changed into His likeness.

Hebrews and Habakkuk

Hebrews is a longer document than Habakkuk and much more carefully worked out. Furthermore, it shows that fullness of thought that comes with Jesus, the incarnate God who provides a substitutionary death for our sins.

Nevertheless, key ideas link the two books.

1. *The sanctuary theme.* Habakkuk 2:20 reminds us, "The Lord is in his holy temple; let all the earth keep silence before him." This thought is not developed in Habakkuk, but in Hebrews it becomes a major idea. "Now the point in what we are saying is this: we have such a high priest, one who is seated at the right hand of the throne of the Majesty in heaven, a minister in the sanctuary and the true tent which is set up not by man but by the Lord" (Heb. 8:1, 2).

2. *The life of faith.* We noticed how Habakkuk 2:4 set forth the ringing statement "the righteous shall live by his faith." Hebrews 10:37, 38 picks up this idea and quotes the verse, but in a wider context than that of Habakkuk's setting. Whereas Habakkuk was troubled by the violence and injustice that he saw around him and by God's prediction of the invasion of the Babylonians, the Hebrew Christians, weary in the spiritual way, had begun to wonder why Jesus had not come back. The answer to both sets of problems is the same—living by faith.

3. *Confidence in the Lord.* Despite the devastation that was to come upon his land, at the end of his book Habakkuk breathes superlative confidence: "Though the fig tree do not blossom, nor fruit be on the vines, the produce of the olive fail and the fields yield no food, the flock be cut off from the fold and there be no herd in the stalls, yet I will rejoice in the Lord, I will joy in the God of my salvation" (Hab. 3:17, 18). Hebrews, as we have suggested above, likewise expresses absolute confidence in Christ. Because of His sinless life and sacrificial death, Jesus has opened a new and living way into the very presence of God. No longer need we be a priest to come into His presence. No longer need we bring a sacrificial animal. No longer need we come in fear and trembling. The way is open to all. Jesus has flung wide the doors of the Temple, which will receive every soul who accepts God's gracious provision.

The God Who Speaks

[Heb. 1:1-4]

One of the saddest developments of our twentieth century is the loss of a sense of meaning. With all his learning, modern man is unable to arrive at a knowledge of the truth. The more he becomes aware of the intricacy of the universe—the more he masters the details of nature and the heavens—the less his sense of an overriding purpose or cause.

This sense of being alone in the universe was eloquently summed up by the British philosopher Bertrand Russell. "That man is the product of causes which had no prevision of the end they were achieving; that his origin, his growth, his hopes and fears, his loves and beliefs, are but the outcome of accidental collocations of atoms; that no fire, no heroism, no intensity of thought and feeling, can preserve an individual life beyond the grave; that all the labours of the ages, all the inspiration, all the noon-day brightness of human genius, are destined to extinction in the vast death of the solar system, and that the whole temple of man's achievement must inevitably be buried beneath the debris of a universe in ruins—all these things, if not quite beyond dispute, are yet so nearly certain, that no philosophy which rejects them can hope to stand. Only within the scaffolding of these truths, only on the firm foundations of unyielding despair, can the soul's habitation henceforth be safely built."—H. J. Paton, *The Modern Predicament*, p. 108.

The book of Hebrews sets forth a startling alternative to this view of life. Its opening words, which like an overture set forth the leading themes of the book, declare two great facts:

There is a God, and He speaks.

"In many and various ways God spoke of old to our fathers by the prophets; but in these last days he has spoken to us by a Son, whom he appointed the heir of all things, through whom also he created the world. He reflects the glory of God and bears the very stamp of his nature, upholding the universe by his word of power. When he had made purification for sins, he sat down at the right hand of the Majesty on high, having become as much superior to angels as the name he has obtained is more excellent than theirs" (Heb. 1:1-4).

Notice that the apostle makes no attempt to prove the existence of God. Although down through the ages philosophers have posited various arguments—arguments based on the design of the universe, our moral sense, the idea of a perfect being, and so on—in the final analysis God can neither be proved nor disproved. Nor does the Bible anywhere attempt to prove the existence of God. The Scriptures simply commence: "In the beginning God created the heavens and the earth" (Gen. 1:1). Instead of trying to prove God by philosophical argument, the Bible invites: "O taste and see that the Lord is good!" (Ps. 34:8). God may be known by personal experience, and for the one who knows, proof is not necessary.

But this great God who fills the universe and who is ultimately beyond puny human minds is a God who speaks. This is the second affirmation of Hebrews 1:1-4. God does not leave us alone—in our silence, in our pain. He might have done so, dwelling in eternal mystery. But because He is Love, He speaks. Love communicates. Love breaks the silence. Love takes the initiative. Love reaches across the void of infinity to make contact with humanity. Our God is a God who speaks.

Hebrews 1:1-4 is rich in theological insights. Apart from what it says about God Himself, we find the following doctrines: revelation and inspiration, cosmology, eschatology, and soteriology. Obviously, we might take each of these themes and explore it at some length. Such a study would occupy many pages. Instead, we shall confine ourselves to the two great ideas of Hebrews 1:1-4—God, and the speaking of God.

God

One of the first impressions the reader of Hebrews takes from the book is the predominance of Christology. Now, while it is true that Christology—especially in the development of Jesus as heavenly high priest—is a major thrust of the writing, we should not overlook a surprising amount of data relative to God. We are apt to overlook this evidence because it is nowhere elaborated; rather, it appears as a continuing backdrop to the Christology.

We note first of all the designations for God. The most common is *theos*, translated always as "God." This term occurs nearly seventy times in the document. Occasionally we find other designations, such as "the majesty on high," (chap. 1:3), "the majesty in heaven" (chap. 8:1), "him who warns" (chap. 12:25), and "the living God" (chaps. 3:12; 9:14; 10:31; 12:22).

Apart from the speaking of God, which we will study later in this chapter, God is set forth in terms of judgment. He is called "a consuming fire" (verse 29), and "judge" (verse 23; chap. 13:4).

God is the source and end of all things. He is the one "for whom and by whom all things exist" (2:10). "He created the world" (chap. 1:2), and all things were "created by the word of God" (chap. 11:3).

He also is the God of promise. He made promises to Abraham (chap. 6:13-18). He stands back of the better promises of the new covenant (chap. 8:6). His promises inspired the heroes of old (chapter 11).

In order to make His promises absolutely sure before humanity, He enters into an oath. Thus He confirmed His promise to Abraham by an oath (chap. 6:13-20), and sent forth Jesus as "surety of a better covenant" (chap. 7:20-22).

Our God is the God of absolute truth. It is impossible for Him to lie (chap. 6:18). What a comforting thought this is! We may take Him at His word, knowing that in Christ Jesus all His promises are Yea and Amen. He stands back of His word that gives us eternal life.

This great God does not remain in infinite remoteness. He draws near to His people. He "is not ashamed to be called their God" (chap. 11:16). He is the one who over and over came to His people in days gone by and who manifested Himself in the supreme event of revelation—the Incarnation.

He also is our heavenly Father, disciplining His children (chap. 12:3-11). Though to us His correction at times seems painful, God acts out of love. Because He is concerned for our well-being, now and eternally, He guides us in the heavenly way.

This God is also able to raise the dead. Abraham trusted in Him as he put the knife to Isaac's throat (chap. 11:19). Although Isaac was delivered from death, Jesus was not. But God showed His ability to bring the dead back to life by raising again the great Shepherd of the sheep, the Lord Jesus (chap. 13:20).

In the book of Hebrews we find several places where God's activities are related to Jesus Christ. Thus, God created all things by the Son (chap. 1:2). He appointed the Son as "heir of all things" (1:2) and designated the Son as high priest (chap. 5:5, 10).

So while Christology is the ruling interest of the author of the book of Hebrews, everywhere we find the divine plan and appointment behind the Son's work in all its phases. The thought is summed up in chapter 3, verse 4: "The builder of all things is God." Thus, Hebrews is a thoroughly theocentric document. Everywhere the person and plan of God overshadow the train of thought. If in almost every place Jesus is in the center stage enjoying the spotlight, God remains in the shadows. Eternal government, the coming of the Son to earth as a man, His living and His dying, His resurrection and ascension, His high priestly ministry, His work of judgment, His second coming—none happens by chance. In all and through all, God is working out His will.

It is also interesting to note what we do *not* find in the book of Hebrews. Jesus' work of intercession is described in a way that avoids a direct reference to God (chap. 7: 25). Likewise, the discussion of the sacrifice of Jesus usually speaks simply of His "offering" of Himself as a sacrifice (verse 27; chaps. 9:11, 12, 24-26; 10:12, 14). In only one place, chapter 9:14, is God mentioned as the referent of the sacrifice (offering) of the Son.

Clearly Hebrews deemphasizes the idea of a dichotomy between the Father and the Son in the salvation of humanity. It avoids that wrong theology which would suggest that the Father and the Son are in some sort of conflict, with the Son interposing His blood or sacrifice. Rather, *all* that happens in the plan of salvation proceeds from God and is of His appointment. This, of course, is just what John 3:16 tells us: *Because* God loved the world He sent His Son to die for the world. He loved the world *before* Jesus died, not simply *because* Jesus died for it.

Especially in our next chapter, and indeed, throughout the remainder of this book, we will observe the person and role of Jesus Christ in the book of Hebrews. Here it is interesting to complete our discussion of the place of God in Hebrews by noting the attention given to the Holy Spirit.

There are six clear references to the Spirit in Hebrews (chaps. 2:4; 3:7; 6:4; 9:8, 14; 10:29). Since God and the Son figure so prominently in the book, we may rightly hold that there is a deemphasis in this document regarding the Holy Spirit. Why? Would not the condition of the readers—sluggish, weary, wavering—lead us to expect an appeal to the Spirit as He who would infuse life and enthusiasm? Rather, the basis of the apostle's appeal is theological. An interesting possibility suggests itself. Hebrews has a consciously anti-"enthusiastic" thrust. It may have been written to counteract an unwarranted emphasis on the place of the Holy Spirit in the congregation in the past.

The Bible clearly sets forth the person and work of the Holy Spirit. The Spirit is eternal and personal, a member of the divine Trinity. He plays a vital role in the plan of salvation. Since the departure of Christ from this earth the Spirit perpetuates His work—convicting of sin, righteous, and judgment (John 16:8-11). The Spirit glorifies Christ, teaching all things and bringing the words of Christ to our remembrance. The Spirit is the divine advocate, the *paraclēte* (literally, one who stands by our side). He is everywhere present and carries on the work of Christ. He woos men and women, leading them to repentance; without Him, no one would come to Christ.

But sometimes the doctrine of the Holy Spirit is misapplied in personal experience. Already in the New Testament we find congregations, such as the one at Corinth, where Christians perpetrated great excesses in the name of the Spirit. Because the Spirit had manifested Himself with an abundance of gifts among the believers, some of those in the congregation had broken over the spiritual traces. They were indifferent to a case of gross immorality in their midst. They were divided into factions and argued among themselves. Their practice of the Lord's Supper had fallen into confusion. They misunderstood and abused Christian freedom.

At times we encounter similar problems today. While many Christians lack for a personal experience of the Spirit, others fall into the opposite extreme. I have encountered men and women who, because they claim to have "received" the Holy Spirit, feel no concern about obeying the claims of God's law, the fourth commandment in particular.

In all such cases, a direct appeal to the Spirit is not the most helpful. We must go back to the Scriptures and give a sound theological base. Experience must be tested and judged by the Word of God; experience must never set itself over against the claims of God's Word.

Perhaps a similar background helps us explain the deemphasis of the role of the Holy Spirit in the book of Hebrews. Perhaps the spiritual condition of the Hebrew Christians—inert, sluggish, tired—corresponds to the reaction from an overheated enthusiasm they had experienced in the past.

God Speaks

Hebrews 1:1-4 sets forth a carefully balanced structure:

Old Testament Speaking	New Testament Speaking
God spoke	God has spoken
to the forefathers	to us
of old	in the last of these days
in (by) the prophets	in the Son
incomplete (many and various ways)	with finality

The Greek text literally reads "God spoke *in* the prophets." That is, God was speaking through the total impact of their lives. As Ellen White has aptly commented concerning the doctrine of inspiration, we should think of inspired men rather than inspired words (see *Selected Messages*, book 1, p. 21).

Hebrews 1:1-4 immediately confronts us with the fact that the Old Testament came from God. At the same time, it points up a sharp contrast—the partial, fragmentary, incomplete character of Old Testament revelation is superseded by the decisive speech of God in the One who is the Son.

Throughout the book of Hebrews we are confronted by the speaking God. God speaks to Abraham (chap. 6:14). He speaks to Israel (chap. 8:8). He speaks to Christ (chap. 5:5). Sometimes it is the Son who speaks (chap. 1:2, 3; 2:12; 10:5). Sometimes it is the Holy Spirit (chap. 3:7). But no matter which member of the Holy Trinity speaks—Father, Son, or Holy Spirit—it is the same Word of God. And that Word of God is the discerner and judge of our innermost thoughts and motives (chap. 4:12, 13).

When God speaks, His word resounds forever. Often in the book of Hebrews we find the present tense: God *speaks.* This idea is underlined by the use of the word *today* (chaps. 3:7, 13, 15; 4:7). "Today" is God's eternal present, which men call "now." Although His word may have been spoken many generations ago, that word is still sounding. It pierces to our conscience, calling us back to the claims of the divine will.

The manner in which the author introduces quotations from the Old Testament further underscores the speaking of God. Nowhere in the book of Hebrews is an Old Testament writer mentioned by name. Always, no matter in what portion of the Old Testament the citation may be found, the speaker is God. This understanding of the Old Testament is in marked contrast to its use in some other New Testament books. For instance: Romans 10:16—"Isaiah says"; Romans 10:19—"Moses says"; Romans 11:9—"David says." But for the writer of Hebrews the Old Testament is *Scripture*—the words are the words of God.

Even where the Old Testament words are clearly the prophet's own words, they are treated as divine words. For example, Hebrews 4:4 quotes Genesis 2:2: "For he has somewhere spoken of the seventh day in this way, 'And God rested on the seventh day from all his works.' " Likewise Hebrews 2:13 quotes Isaiah 8:17, 18. "And again, 'I will put my trust in him.' And again, 'Here am I, and the children God has given me.' " Similarly, Hebrews 13:5 quotes Deuteronomy 31:6. "Keep your life free from love of money, and be content with what you have; for he has said, 'I will never fail you nor forsake you.' "

We notice the contrast with other New Testament documents: Romans 9:15—"*he* says to Moses"; Romans 9:25—"*he* says in Hosea"; 2 Corinthians 6:2—"*God* says."

In only one place does the book of Hebrews refer to a human author, and here the reference is as general as possible: "One has testified somewhere . . ." (Heb. 2:6, N.A.S.B.).

Hebrews' manner of citing the Old Testament is unique among the New Testament books. Usually quotations are introduced by "It is written" (sixteen times in the book of Romans). Occasionally we find them introduced with "The scripture says."

As we look at the actual quotations from the Old Testament, several facts emerge:

1. The Psalms predominate, both in the number of

quotations and the weight the quotations play in the argument. Psalm 110 is especially important, and in particular verse 4 of that psalm—"The Lord has sworn and will not change his mind, you are a priest for ever after the order of Melchizedek."

2. We find no mention or allusion to Isaiah 53. Indeed, in the book of Hebrews we find only three references to the prophetic section of the Old Testament.

3. The apostle usually quotes from the Septuagint, although six quotations differ from both the Septuagint and the Hebrew text.

4. Of particular interest is the manner in which the argument relies on the Septuagint text in several places. The Hebrew text could not sustain it. For example: Hebrews 2:6-8 quotes Psalm 8:4-6. The Hebrew text reads "Thou hast made him but a little lower than God," while the Septuagint has "Thou madest him a little lower than angels" (N.A.S.B.). Hebrews 10:5-7, 10 quotes Psalm 40:6-8. Here the Hebrew text has "ears hast thou digged for me," but the Septuagint has "a body hast thou prepared me."

The use of the Old Testament in the book of Hebrews has evoked much scholarly interest. We have touched on only some of the interesting data here. An especially fascinating area, which we cannot take up in this book, concerns the manner in which passages out of the Old Testament are applied to the person and work of Jesus.

The God who speaks—it is the ruling idea of the book of Hebrews. It tells us:

the *fact* of revelation—God has not left us alone. He has broken the silence. He has spoken; He speaks!

the *abiding* character of His revelation—the words of God are timeless in their force.

the *seriousness* of revelation—to neglect or reject the word of God brings the direst consequences.

the personal *confrontation* of revelation—revelation addresses each hearer directly and incisively, demanding a response today.

the high view of the *inspiration* of the Old Testament—

God speaks, no matter what the identity of the prophet.

the Old Testament is *Messianic* throughout.

No, we cannot prove that there is a God. But we may know Him, know Him personally, know Him as our friend.

No, we cannot prove that God speaks. But we may listen, and if we do we will hear His voice.

The Magnificence of Jesus

[Heb. 1:5-2:18]

Jesus is magnificent—the man of matchless charms, the desire of all nations. In Him we see what it means to be made in the image of God.

"It would be well for us to spend a thoughtful hour each day in contemplation of the life of Christ," Ellen White has counseled. "We should take it point by point, and let the imagination grasp each scene, especially the closing ones. As we thus dwell upon His great sacrifice for us, our confidence in Him will be more constant, our love will be quickened, and we shall be more deeply imbued with His Spirit. If we would be saved at last, we must learn the lesson of penitence and humiliation at the foot of the cross."— *The Desire of Ages*, p. 83.

Jesus Christ dominates the book of Hebrews. Throughout the discussion His person (who He is) and His work (what He does) flow together. His work is significant and efficacious because of who He is, while His person receives even greater honor because of what He has done for us. This is the meaning of the New Testament idea that as a result of His incarnation, sufferings, and death, He is now exalted to a preeminent degree.

Who was Jesus of Nazareth? The people of His day had no question about His humanity. He was a carpenter of Nazareth. His brothers and sisters and Mary and Joseph were known to many. People had watched Him grow up in that notorious town. They had seen Him develop into manhood, known of His toil at the carpenter's bench, and worshiped with Him every Sabbath in the synagogue.

But was He *more* than another man? When He forsook the carpenter's bench and entered upon the life of an itinerant preacher-healer, this question became ever more pressing. At Caesarea Philippi He Himself thrust it upon His disciples: " 'Who do *you* say that I am?' " Throughout the Gospels we see the reaction of men and women to Jesus, with the gradual dawning of the light as individuals here and there came to acknowledge that, yes, Jesus of Nazareth was *more* than another man. And at Caesarea Philippi Peter, inspired by the Holy Spirit, made the blessed confession: " 'You are the Christ, the Son of the living God' " (Matt. 16:16).

The book of Hebrews sets forth the full deity and the full humanity of Jesus in startling contrast. Chapter 1 argues that what God is Jesus is; chapter 2 argues that Jesus became lower than the angels—one with us, our brother, flesh and blood.

We find no explanation as to how this could be. We find no attempt to wrestle with those theological conundrums that would occupy theologians for centuries and lead to name-calling and division and even physical conflict. No explanation—only affirmation.

Those Christians of later times who wrestled with these matters, who argued and quarreled and at last physically fought, might have learned much from the book of Hebrews. They might have heeded its implied suggestion that ultimately the person of Jesus Christ eludes complete human explanation. In speaking of the Incarnation, we are speaking about God. And God cannot be encompassed within the mind of humanity.

Let us, then, notice how decisively Hebrews sets forth the deity of Jesus. Then let us notice how decisively it sets forth the complete humanity of Jesus. And, finally, let us see where the argument leads us: how this unique combination of God and man brings us salvation.

Jesus, Fully God

No writer of the New Testament sets forth a higher

Christology than the author of Hebrews. With some notable exceptions, the writers of the New Testament shrink from directly attributing deity to Jesus. Instead, they use terms such as *Messiah, Son of David,* or *Son of God* that point in the direction of deity without precisely saying so.

Not so the book of Hebrews. In chapter 1, verse 3 we read: "He reflects the glory of God and bears the very stamp of his nature, upholding the universe by his word of power." Three terms here are especially significant.

1. Christ "reflects the glory of God." The Greek term is *apaugasma,* which means "radiance, effulgence, or reflection." This expression points to the Son's manifestation of the divine attributes—He is like the ray or beam of the sun.

2. He is "the very stamp of His nature." Here the Greek word is *charaktēr,* which means "impress, reproduction, or representation." Our familiar word *character* derives from this source. The Greek term points to an impress used in engraving, such as the impression or stamp on coins and seals. In Hebrews 1:3 the expression shows that the Son is the stamp of the divine nature, being, or essence. Thus, it indicates representative traits, not absolute identity of the Son with the Father.

3. In the Greek Hebrews 1:1-4 is one unbroken sentence. Verse three is introduced by the Greek word *ōn,* which is literally "being." That is, the apostle is telling us that the Son whom he has introduced in verse 2 is the one who *is* the reflection of God's glory and the very stamp of His nature. This little term *ōn* is deeply significant. It assures that Christ did not *become* the reflection of the divine glory or the stamp of the divine essence. Rather, the Son *always* was these, *always* is these.

By this little word Christian theology is protected from those conceptions of Jesus that, arising early in Christian history, suggested that He was not eternally equal to God. At the Council of Nicea, called in A.D. 325, this particular issue was at the forefront. The protagonists were Arius and Athanasius. The critical issue was "Was there a time when the Son was not?" Arius' answer was Yes. Athanasius' answered, No. On the basis of Hebrews 1:3 and other New Testament scriptures, we may affirm that Athanasius' position was the correct one—the Son eternally was equal with God. He is without beginning and without end.

We should give some consideration to the key term *Son* in the book of Hebrews. In our usual human experience Son does not point to equality. Instead, it signifies descent—a Son is never as old as the parent. We should beware of reading this meaning into the Biblical usage, however. In each occurrence of the word *Son* in the book of Hebrews as applied to Jesus Christ, we find particular weight given to the term.

Chapter 1:2—"One who is Son" indicates the superior quality of the new revelation.

Chapter 1:8—"The Son" is contrasted with angels.

Chapter 3:56—Moses is a servant, whereas Christ is a Son.

Chapter 4:14—Christ is a great high priest because He is the Son.

Chapter 5:5—Christ's appointment as high priest is made on the basis that He is the divine Son.

Chapter 5:8—"Although he was a Son," He suffered the agony of Gethsemane in obedience to the divine will.

Chapter 6:6—There is no repentance for those who crucify again the Son of God.

Chapter 7:3—Melchizedek is "like unto the Son of God" (K.J.V.).

Chapter 7:28—Our high priest is one who is the Son.

Chapter 10:29—Judgment awaits those who trample underfoot the blood of the Son of God.

The term *Son*, then, clearly points to the surpassing dignity of Christ. All that God is, He is. He is never to be placed on a merely human level. Sonship qualifies Him to be high priest. He, not Melchizedek, is the criterion of the new priesthood. It is because He is Son that the spurning of His sacrifice is heinous.

Is the Sonship of Jesus related to the plan of salvation, or is it eternal? Is it related to the Incarnation, or is He the preincarnate Son?

A study of Hebrews 1:1-4 strongly suggests that "Son" is an eternal designation. It indicates oneness of nature, not origin. In this regard John 5:18 is instructive: "This was why the Jews sought all the more to kill him, because he not only broke the sabbath but also called God his own Father, making himself equal with God." Clearly, for the Jews of Jesus' day, this calling God His Father expressed equality with the Father.

Ellen White likewise has several instructive comments that bear on the eternal Sonship of Jesus:

"Christ is the pre-existent, self-existent Son of God."— *Evangelism*, p. 615.

"He is the eternal, self-existent Son."—*Ibid.*

"The Word existed as a divine being, even as the eternal Son of God, in union and oneness with His Father."—*Ibid.*

Thus, the designation "Son" for Jesus Christ in the book of Hebrews seems to point to His eternal deity. It is a statement of those mysterious relationships that defy human analysis—those within the being of God Himself.

If any should still not be satisfied as to the Son's full deity, in two places the book of Hebrews specifically addresses the Son as God: chapter 1:8—"But of the Son he says, 'Thy throne, O God, is for ever and ever' "; chapter 1:10—" 'Thou, Lord, didst found the earth in the beginning, and the heavens are the work of thy hands.' "

Jesus, Fully Man

Hebrews 1, John 1, Colossians 1, Revelation 1—these chapters set out the highest Christology in the New Testament. In Hebrews, however, the presentation is immediately followed by a portrayal of Jesus' humanity in the starkest terms.

Hebrews 2 confronts us with the *fact* of His humanity. Chapter 2:9 tells us that He became "a little while . . . lower than the angels." In order to catch the force of the argument we need to remember that in chapter 1, verses 4-14 Christ had been set forth as higher than the angels. But, says the apostle, the humiliation of Jesus to a position lower than that of any angel was but a temporary thing. It was confined to "the days of his flesh" (chap. 5:7).

The entire second chapter of Hebrews underscores the fact of Jesus' humanity. He is called our brother (verses 11-14). He partakes of flesh and blood (verse 14). He is made like His brothers (verse 17). He suffers (verse 10), dies (verses 9, 14), and is tested in all points (verse 18; chap. 4:15).

Many Jews of the first century highly regarded angels. But the book of Hebrews shows that Jesus is greater than any angel. They are created beings; He is not. They worship Him. They serve Him. Unlike Him, God nowhere addresses them as "Son."

To the apostle's teaching about Jesus' deity, the Jewish critic might have responded: "Your reasoning is ridiculous. Look at Jesus of Nazareth—a man, and one who died on a cross! He wasn't even *equal* to the angels!"

But in Hebrews 2 the writer effectively counters any such reasoning. He argues that Jesus' status as lower than the angels was but for a limited time. He then goes on to show that the Incarnation was *necessary* for the plan of salvation. By becoming human, Jesus won for us magnificent victories that could not have been possible had He chosen to remain eternally apart from humanity.

Thus, in chapter 2:10 we read: "For it was fitting that he, for whom and by whom all things exist, in bringing many sons to glory, should make the pioneer of their salvation perfect through suffering." Likewise at verse 17 we read: "He *had* to be made like his brethren in every respect." The humanity of Jesus, therefore, is to be understood on the basis of necessity and appropriateness.

And what did He accomplish, according to Hebrews 2:5-18?

1. *He tasted death for us all (verse 9).* He died in our place, entering into the experience of desolation and rejection that the Scriptures term "the second death."

The famous preacher Chrysostom of the early church commented thus on Christ's tasting death: "Moreover He said rightly *taste* death for every man'; He did not say 'die.' For as if He really was *tasting* it when He had spent but a little time therein, He immediately rose. . . . For as a physician, though not needing to taste the food prepared for the sick man, yet in his care for him tastes first himself, that he may persuade the sick man with confidence to venture on the food; so, since all men were afraid of death, in persuading them to take courage against death, He tasted it also Himself, though He needed not."

As great a preacher and expositor as Chrysostom was, he surely misunderstood Hebrews 2:10. Christ's *tasting* of death denotes the intensity of the experience, the bitterness of the cup that He accepted from the Father's hand. J. McLeod Campbell is closer to the mark: "When I think of our Lord as tasting death it seems to me as if He alone ever truly tasted death."—*The Nature of the Atonement*, p. 259.

2. *He became one with humanity (verse 11).* Our concerns became His concerns; our pain became His pain; our joy became His joy. Some may argue that since God knows all things, the Incarnation could add nothing to God's knowledge. The book of Hebrews leads us in a different direction: It suggests that knowledge born of experience can be achieved in no other way, so that in a peculiar and beautiful way the Godhead is now joined to humanity by ties that did not exist before and that now can never be broken.

Ellen White has made this very point: "By His life and His death, Christ has achieved even more than recovery from the ruin wrought through sin. It was Satan's purpose to bring about an eternal separation between God and man; but in Christ we become more closely united to God than if we had never fallen. In taking our nature, the Saviour has bound Himself to humanity by a tie that is never to be broken. Through the eternal ages He is linked with us. 'God so loved the world, that he gave his only-begotten Son' (John 3:16). He gave Him not only to bear our sins, and to die as our sacrifice; He gave Him to the fallen race. To assure us of His immutable counsel of peace, God gave His only-begotten

Son to become one of the human family, forever to retain His human nature. This is the pledge that God will fulfill His word. 'Unto *us* a child is born, unto *us* a son is given: and the government shall be upon his shoulder.' God has adopted human nature in the person of His Son, and has carried the same into the highest heaven. It is the 'Son of man' who shares the throne of the universe. It is the 'Son of man' whose name shall be called, 'Wonderful, Counselor, The mighty God, The everlasting Father, The Prince of Peace' (Isa. 9:6). The I AM is the Daysman between God and humanity, laying His hand upon both. He who is 'holy, harmless, undefiled, separate from sinners,' is not ashamed to call us brethren (Heb. 7: 26; 2:11). In Christ the family of earth and the family of heaven are bound together. Christ glorified is our brother. Heaven is enshrined in humanity, and humanity is enfolded in the bosom of Infinite Love."—*The Desire of Ages*, pp. 25, 26.

One with us, Jesus suffered and was tempted (chap. 2:10, 18). There was no make-believe in His experiences. He was not an actor in a divine charade, pretending to be one with us, looking human, but knowing from the beginning how everything would work out. No, He risked failure and eternal loss. His temptations were real temptations, His struggles real struggles.

3. *By His humanity Jesus broke the power of death (verses 14, 15)*. Because He became man, He could enter the realm of death—and defeat it from within!

The inscriptions on the tombs from the first century tell a pathetic story. "Farewell, my friend, I'll never see you again." "Goodbye, Alexamenos, it's all over." They portray the hopelessness, grief, and sense of eternal loss. But into that first-century world came a new message. Christianity proclaimed that One had burst the bonds of the tomb! It preached Jesus Christ, conqueror of heaven and earth, conqueror of the grave! It preached deliverance—deliverance for those facing death and deliverance for the living—deliverance from the bondage of the fear of death!

What a message for our day also! Writings of the great

men and women of our century breathe a spirit of despair and hopelessness, of frustration at the thought of impending death. Sartre, Camus, Hemingway—for them all life is, as Hemingway put it, a "dirty joke." The last laugh is nothingness.

The message of Jesus' empty tomb is just as much needed in our generation. And it is just as powerful. We proclaim a living Saviour, one whom the kingdom of death could not hold in its sway.

4. *The climax of chapter 2, however, comes in its closing verses.* "Therefore he had to be made like his brethren in every respect, so that he might become a merciful and faithful high priest in the service of God, to make expiation for the sins of the people" (verse 17). Because of the Incarnation *Jesus is qualified to be our heavenly high priest.*

Note the two aspects brought out in verse 17. First, Jesus was not eternally high priest. Because of the Incarnation He *became* high priest. Second, by becoming human and dying on the cross, He provided a sacrifice for sin.

These two great ideas—the high priestly ministry of Jesus Christ and His all-sufficient sacrifice provided on Calvary—are the great themes of the book of Hebrews. They will shape the discussion over the next eight chapters.

Song of the Pilgrim

[Heb. 3:1-4:13]

High in the Himalayas I have seen bands of men and women making their way along mountain trails to the headwaters of the sacred Ganges or Jumna. They wear the holy marks of the Hindu religion on their wrists and foreheads; small bundles of possessions are tied to their backs; they have staves in their hands to help them negotiate the rocky paths.

They are pilgrims who have left their homes, perhaps hundreds of miles away, and set out on a religious journey. The light in their eyes and the fervor of their countenances tell of the inner quest that has brought them to the Himalayas. They have a purpose, a goal, and they will not be deterred by the difficulties along the way.

The idea of pilgrimage means less and less to Western man. Our modern concept is a vague amalgam of Pilgrim Fathers, *Canterbury Tales*, and *Pilgrim's Progress.* How inexact the term is today we can see by the wide-ranging definitions listed in *Webster's Third New International Dictionary of the English Language,* unabridged: "A journey of a pilgrim; especially one to a shrine or a sacred place. . . the act of making such a journey . . . a trip taken to visit a place of historic or sentimental interest or to participate in a specific event or for a definite purpose . . . the course of life on earth . . . a particular part of the life course of an individual . . . a search for mental and spiritual values."

Such a bland, generalized view of pilgrimage offers little help to us. Our secular twentieth century has lost the fundamental religious idea of pilgrimage. In fact, we have so compromised it that we no longer can describe a pilgrim with clarity. Nevertheless, traces of the pilgrim idea remain. We still sing the old hymns, "Guide me, O Thou great Jehovah! Pilgrim through this barren land," "O happy band of pilgrims," and "I'm a pilgrim, and I'm a stranger."

Especially in the book of Hebrews we find instruction that clarifies the concept of Christian pilgrimage. Chapters 3 and 4, and later chapter 11, remind us in no uncertain terms that this world is not our final home. God designs that we shall not set our values and aspirations on the things of this earth. Although this world is good—after all, it is *His* world, because He made it—we were made to live eternally in the presence of God. We must not become so engrossed with the things of this life, with getting and spending that, as Wordsworth put it, "we lay waste our powers." We must set our sights on the heavenly goal. We must realize that this life, be it short or long, is designed by God to be part of a journey—our pilgrimage—to the better land.

In Hebrews 3:1-4:13 the pilgrim idea is a leading theme. Although the word *pilgrim* itself does not occur, the apostle underscores the idea of Christian life as being *on the march.* He draws many lessons from Israel's wandering in the wilderness for forty years—always moving, but never arriving. And he warns us lest we, having started well as Christians, should likewise fall short of the final goal.

The passage is rich in theological, practical, and exegetical insights. We shall devote our attention to three of its great ideas—our leader, our journey, and our promised rest.

Our Leader

The first six verses of chapter 3 direct us to "consider Jesus, the high priest and apostle of our confession." The author compares Him with Moses, Israel's leader during the forty years of wandering. He will reason that Christ and Moses are similar in terms of their faithfulness, but that Christ is superior to Moses.

For three reasons, Christ is greater than Moses:

1. Moses was faithful *in* his house, but Christ was faithful *over* His house. Just as the builder of a house is much more worthy than the house itself, so Christ is greater than Moses. That is, Moses is viewed by the apostle as being part of the house.

2. Moses was a servant, but Christ is a Son.

3. Moses and Christ stand in relation as promise and fulfillment: Moses was a witness to the revelation to come in Jesus Christ.

Why this concern to show that Jesus is greater than Moses?

Possibly because rabbinical tradition, commenting on Numbers 12:7, "Not so with my servant Moses; he is entrusted with all my house," had put Moses higher than angels. The rabbis said, "God calls Moses 'faithful in all his house,' and thereby he ranked higher than the ministering angels themselves."

The second reason for the contrast is possibly because of the two revelations: As Moses was the supreme figure in the old revelation, so Christ is the supreme figure in the new. This line of reasoning, as we have already noticed in the first two chapters of Hebrews, underscores the magnificence of the Christian religion. And that in turn drives home the apostle's warning about the peril of neglecting or rejecting the blessings that have come to us in Jesus Christ.

We should not set out the contrast between Moses and Christ in terms of Moses' failure to lead his people into the Promised Land. Indeed, in chapter 3 and throughout the book of Hebrews, we find no disparagement of Moses. Further, the apostle specifically states that the failure to enter the Promised Land was a result of the people's rebellion and disobedience (chaps. 3:16, 18; 4:6). He likewise warns his Christian readers that they too may fail to enter the rest that the Lord has prepared for them—even though Christ is their leader! (chap. 4:1, 11).

Think of the blessings of ancient Israel. Think of the mighty acts of God that led them out from Egypt—the series of plagues, the judgment on the firstborn sons of Egypt, the parting of the Red Sea. Think also of the miraculous way by which God led them through that burning, arid wilderness. Surely God had brought them out with a mighty hand and had done wonders in their midst.

Think also of the leader He raised up. Moses, saved at birth from the decree of a ruthless king, was raised in the court of Pharaoh. He was skilled in the learning of the Egyptians and in their martial arts. And after a period of forty years of education in the finest schools of his day, God sent him into the desert for another forty years for him to learn the wisdom of the Eternal. At last he was ready for the task to which God had called him. Now he was humble and meek, no longer trusting in his wisdom and physical strength. He was, the Scriptures say, the meekest man "on the face of the earth" (Num. 12:3). He was a man whom God could use!

In view of God's mighty acts, in view of the leader He provided, did not the children of Israel fail abysmally? What more could God have done for them to ensure that they would make it through to the land of Canaan? And yet—dare we be too hard on God's people of that generation? Are we any better than they?

Think of the mighty acts of God in Christian history. Those mighty acts, let us never forget, begin with the life, death, and resurrection of Jesus Christ. And they extend through the years of our church's history. They embrace His calling forth from the world a little band of people that has grown, against all odds, into a worldwide movement embracing every nation, kindred, tongue, and people.

Let's look at a few examples.

The Lord gave us the health message. Today we have more than five hundred hospitals and clinics worldwide. Adventist health services are known in many lands for their quality and farsightedness. In the United States alone, we have more than seventy health institutions with assets of about $1.6 billion.

The Lord gave us an educational message. Today we have the largest Protestant school system worldwide.

The Lord gave us a publishing message. Today we

operate fifty-one publishing houses that print in 175 languages, with annual sales of more than $120 million.

Surely God has been good to His Adventist people in these last days! And beyond all His marvelous leadings, what a Leader! Not Moses, the meekest man on the face of the earth, but Jesus Christ, the God-man!

Let us therefore not disparage ancient Israel. Let us humble ourselves and search our hearts and beware lest we also fail to attain the promised goal.

The Journey

In Hebrews 3:7-19 the apostle draws at some length on the wanderings of Israel in the wilderness. His discussion turns on the quotation of Psalm 95:7-11. Psalm 95 itself falls into two parts: a call to worship (verses 1-7), and a warning against disobeying God (last part of verse 7 through 11). The psalm has a long connection with the Sabbath, being one of the special psalms inaugurated for the Sabbath. Perhaps it goes back to the tabernacle service on the Sabbath.

Expounding on Psalm 95, the apostle shows that the entire forty years in the desert were a "day of temptation" (verse 8, K.J.V.) during which the people exasperated God. In searching analysis he points out the steps that led to Israel's failure. He identifies the "evil, unbelieving heart" (verse 12), the falling away from serving God (verse 12), the gradual hardening of the heart (verse 13), the seduction because of the deceitfulness of sin (verse 13), the loss of first confidence in the Lord's leading (verse 14), and eventually overt rebellion (verse 16).

The hardening of the heart is especially suggestive. Spiritual atherosclerosis—what a terrible end! The most alarming aspect of it is that, like actual atherosclerosis, the disease proceeds without the person's being aware that his life force is gradually being constricted.

Metallurgy provides an interesting parallel. High-quality steels under the microscope show a beautiful crystalline structure. These metals can be softened by heat and made into new configurations. They can be softened and hardened and reworked many times. But not indefinitely. A point is reached when the crystalline structure of the metal becomes permanently set, and it refuses to conform to further treatment.

So in the spiritual life. Although the Lord is long-suffering with us and the Spirit never ceases to plead, a point of no return lies somewhere down the road of everybody's life. Spiritual atherosclerosis can eventually so block our channels to the Lord that He is no longer able to make contact with us.

Another key word is *sēmeron*—"today." This word, also taken directly out of Psalm 95, comes with unusual directness. It is, as the poet Browning said, "God's instant men called years." Today is the time of divine call and divine opportunity. Today is the moment to take stock of who we are, where we are, and whither we are tending. Today is the moment to hearken to God's voice. Today is the day of opportunity!

So Israel's journey dragged on and on. The forty years in the wilderness were a far longer time than God ever intended. He did not fail; the people failed. The generation that Moses had led out of Egypt had to fall in the desert before God could bring Israel through to the Promsed Land.

Israel's failure is summed up in a word that occurs twice in this chapter—*unbelief* (verses 12, 19). In the Greek this word is *apistia*, literally "unfaith." In order to catch the force of this word, we should see its relationship to other words from the same root.

In verse 2 Christ is called faithful—*pistos*. Moses also is called *pistos* (verses 2, 5). Whereas Jesus and Moses were both characterized by faithfulness, Israel suffered from lack of faith. In chapter 4, verse 2, this idea becomes explicit: "For good news came to us just as to them; but the message which they heard did not benefit them, because it did not meet with faith in the hearers."

Faith is a leading word of the book of Hebrews. As we shall see in our discussion of Hebrews 11, faith marked the experience of the great men and women in days of old. And it is the mark of the pilgrim today.

The Promised Rest

In chapter 4 the apostle turns from Israel's experience to modern Israel—the Christians. They are not on the way to the earthly Canaan, but they nonetheless are pilgrims on the journey to the heavenly Jerusalem.

Chapter 4, verses 1-10 is a tightly reasoned passage. As we seek to understand it, three issues confront us:

1. What is the "rest" of which the apostle speaks?

2. What is the time of the rest: Is it present or future?

3. What is the argument concerning works in verse 10? Specifically, what are the works that the one who enters into rest is to give up, and what is their relation to God's works?

Before we take up each of these questions in turn, we should notice the manner in which the argument is built up:

1. Only two generations are now in view, the wilderness one and the generation at the time of the writing of the book of Hebrews. The apostle has passed over the intervening period to sharpen the point of comparison.

2. Both of these generations have been given marvelous opportunities. Both have received the gospel, and God has provided "rest" for each.

3. God's part is complete. The "rest" has been provided from the foundation of the world. Therefore, failure to enter rest must be placed squarely at the feet of the people—because of a lack of faithfulness.

4. God's promise to enter rest remains unfulfilled. This is especially the point made in verses 6 and 7. The reasoning here is that Psalm 95, written in the time of David, sets forth the rest as still being unfulfilled. Therefore, the "today" at the time of the psalm refers to a later period.

5. Basic to the reasoning is the idea that the promise of God *must* find fulfillment. "Therefore it remains for some to enter it" (verse 6).

6. But the existence of the promise and the establishment by God of His "rest" does not guarantee that any *particular* people will enter it. If God's promise must find

fulfillment, it does not necessarily have to be in and through us. Like the Israelites of old, we may, by our unbelief, nullify for us His promise and provision.

With these points as a basis, we are ready to examine the three questions we outlined above.

What is the rest referred to in chapter 4? Expositors suggest various possibilities—the earthly Canaan, the heavenly Canaan, the spiritual rest in Jesus Christ, the Sabbath, even Sunday!

We note first of all the interchangeability of the words used for rest. In verses 1, 3, 4, 5, 8, and 10, the word for rest is *katapausis.* In verse 9 we find an abrupt change to *sabbatismos.* However, verses 1, 6, and 9 seem clearly to be parallel in expression:

Verse 1: a rest remains.

Verse 6: a rest remains.

Verse 9: a Sabbath rest remains.

Thus, in Hebrews 4:1-10, it seems indisputable that *katapausis* and *sabbatismos* are being used interchangeably. This, however, does not mean that *katapausis* is used throughout chapters 3:6-4:13 with the same meaning. Indeed, we see a development of meaning. If we had only chapter 3, we would not have thought of any meaning beyond that of earthly Canaan, for this was the clear intent of the divine oath on the disobedient Israelites—they would never get into the Promised Land.

But chapter 4 enlarges the idea of rest. The writer argues that even Joshua's generation, which entered Canaan, did not fulfill the promise, because Psalm 95 was written during the time of David. Significantly, he locates the rest prior to the generation of the Israelites; he goes back to the very beginning of the world. Further, he specifically relates it to the Sabbath rest given at the close of Creation week. Finally, he relates this rest to God's rest after His work of Creation was complete.

Thus, the apostle shows that he intends a spiritualizing of rest. He is not referring to Canaan. To make his argument clear, he uses a new word, very likely coining it himself—

sabbatismos. This word is found nowhere else in the Greek New Testament, nor in secular Greek writings. Indeed, not for a century after the book of Hebrews do we find another occurrence of this word.

That is the rest of which the apostle speaks in chapter 4:1-10, the rest that is his concern for Christians, is a "Sabbath rest," a "Sabbathlike rest." This means it is a rest that is like God's own rest after Creation was complete, a rest which the Sabbath itself resembles.

What, then, is the time of this rest?

We find strong indications for the present. In verse 3 he uses the present tense—"We who have believed *enter.*" He also argues that the rest *is:*

Verse 3: available from the beginning of the world.

Verses 1, 6, 9: it "remains."

This means that the rest is not something to be realized in the future at God's appointed time. Further, the force of "today" carries a strong emphasis on the present. Finally, the tense used in verse 10—"hath *ceased* from his own works" (K.J.V.)—rather than "shall cease from His works," as might be argued for a future reference—suggests the rest as something realized in the present.

These points are persuasive, but they fall short of absolute conclusiveness. It is possible to think of the present tense as having futuristic significance. Even the idea of the rest "remaining" does not cancel out the possibility of the heavenly Canaan awaiting those who are faithful. We also should not divorce the discussion in chapter 4:1-10 from the verses that precede the passage in chapter 3. The illustration of Israel wandering toward the earthly Canaan suggests a generation of Christians on their way to the heavenly Canaan.

Here is the crux of the discussion: Is the "rest" of chapter 4:1 to be equated with "the world to come" of chapter 2:5 and "the city" to come of chapters 11:10, 13-16, and 13:14? If so, it seems undeniable that the future sense is to be given prime place in the interpretation.

On balance, we must give force to the tenses as we find

them. This means that the present aspect is uppermost in the interpretation. This idea, too, finds support in the letter elsewhere: The theme of what Christ already has accomplished is surely the major one. The idea of resting in the all-sufficient work of Calvary is not to be played down.

But we should add that such an interpretation does not in itself necessarily exclude the future aspect. The believer even now may enter into the rest of God provided in Christ and yet await the fullness of rest in the heavenly Canaan.

What are our works from which we cease when we enter rest?

In verse 10 the apostle draws an analogy between the person who enters God's rest and God's creative activity. However, we need to note carefully the point of His analogy. It cannot be in the works themselves, since God's works are good while ours are bad. Rather, the analogy is made in terms of the *cessation* from works. Here alone is the point he is stressing.

The works from which a person ceases when he enters God's rest, then, must be the antithesis of the way he enters rest. The way to enter rest, we have already seen from verses 2 and 3, is faith. The antithesis of this way is unbelief—that faithlessness that issues in disobedience.

Here, then, is the concept of rest in Hebrews 4. "Rest" is that blessedness and peace that the Christian receives when he rests wholly on the Lord and from which issue forth faith and obedience. This experience will reach its totality and consummation in the future when the pilgrim at last reaches the heavenly Canaan.

As a parenthesis we should notice the relation of verse 9 to the Sabbath. This verse has been set forth as a proof text for both Sunday and Sabbath. How much can be argued from it?

1. It is clear that the day of worship is not the issue at all. The "rest" transcends a particular day's observance.

2. Likewise it is manifest that not a shred of support for Sundaykeeping is to be found here. Rather the Sabbath is placed in a highly favorable context. It is a type of the rest

that Christians are to seek. We find no suggestion of a change in the day of worship.

3. Underlying the whole discussion is the assumption that the Christians addressed were keeping the Sabbath. Thus, verse 9 brings in the Sabbath in an unstudied way, and so it is a strong support for Sabbathkeeping in the early church.

Our Great High Priest

[Heb. 4:14-5:10; 7:1-28]

When the writer of the book of Hebrews introduces Jesus as high priest (chap. 2:17), he does so without explanation or elaboration. This suggests that the early Christians were already familiar with the idea. But as we search through the New Testament we find that in no book apart from Hebrews is Jesus explicitly called high priest—although references to His intercession and heavenly ministry are found elsewhere (e.g., Rom. 8:34; Rev. 1:12-18; 5:1-14).

It is clear that Jesus as high priest is a leading thought of Hebrews. After seven chapters of theological argumentation the apostle sums up his work: "Now this is my main point: just such a high priest we have, and he has taken his seat at the right hand of the throne of Majesty in the heavens, a ministrant in the real sanctuary, the tent pitched by the Lord and not by man" (chap. 8:1, 2, N.E.B.).

But the idea of the high priesthood of Jesus is not one that is readily understandable to modern people. For a start, we have little to do with priests, temples, and sacrifices. In some parts of the world religious people offer animal sacrifices, as in the temple to Kali in Calcutta. Brahmins preside over the temple complexes of India, some of them vast, highly organized, and fabulously wealthy. Shamans propitiate African deities with bloody sacrifices. But for us in the West, with our Protestant tradition, the priestly concept is remote. For long we have lived on the Reformation's principle of the priesthood of believers.

So the reasoning of the book of Hebrews leaves many Christians and some Adventists cold. They simply do not see its significance for our life today. And when they want to cite an example of obscure Biblical logic they may refer to the Melchizedek passage in chapter 7.

But I contend that the priestly argumentation of Hebrews is both understandable and valuable to Christians today. We should remember that Hebrews is a sermon, not a piece of cryptic writing, and that the original readers surely understood the book. We certainly need to concentrate in order to understand it, but if we apply ourselves, the Holy Spirit will lead us to grasp its essential truths.

In this chapter I shall try to show the importance of this great idea of the book of Hebrews—Jesus as our high priest. Without opening up all the arguments that lie between the first mention of Jesus as our high priest and the summary statement of chapter 8:1, 2, I shall outline the greatness of our High Priest, His superiority to the Aaronic priests, and His superiority to Melchizedek.

The Greatness of Jesus

Hebrews 4:14-16 opens up the topic for us: "Since therefore we have a great high priest who has passed through the heavens, Jesus the Son of God, let us hold fast to the religion we profess. For ours is not a high priest unable to sympathize with our weaknesses, but one who, because of his likeness to us, has been tested every way, only without sin. Let us therefore boldly approach the throne of our gracious God, where we may receive mercy and in his grace find timely help" (N.E.B.).

Why is Jesus called "great"?

First, because of His access to God. He has passed through the heavens—that is, reached the very right hand of God. This indicates that the barriers that separate humanity from God have been broken down.

Second, our High Priest is Jesus, the Son of God! Here is no Aaron, no Moses, not even a Melchizedek. The dignity of His office corresponds to the exalted name He bears.

But these two points could well lead us to think of the remoteness of our great High Priest. He is remote from us in location and superior in name. Here is where verse 16 comes in. Despite His greatness, Jesus is a sympathetic high priest.

The help that Jesus is able to give is superior because:

1. He has been tempted in all things. He knows the heat of the tempter's trials. His tests extend beyond ours because we have yielded before temptation has run its full course, whereas He has never yielded.

2. Through it all He was without sin. The best help, as Moffatt rightly says, is "that afforded by those who have stood where we slip and face the onset of temptation without yielding to it."

So we see the conclusion of the matter in verse 16—we have boldness to come to God. In the writings of Philo Judeaus, contemporary of Jesus, the word *boldness*, *parrēsia*, was the reward of a good conscience. The Roman philosopher Seneca advised people to pray boldly if their desires were such as that they would not be ashamed to have others hear them.

But for Hebrews, boldness is something quite different. Our *parrēsia* is in the throne of grace. Grace has now been enthroned! Unlike the Old Testament sanctuary, where the worshiper waited outside the tent as the Levitical priest entered the first apartment and the high priest alone and on one day a year broke through the barriers of the system to reach the mercy seat, we each may come boldly to the throne of grace.

The greatest barrier between man and God is sin. By His sacrifice Christ has removed this barrier. Now we have direct access to God.

At a stroke this argument cuts away all those religious ordinances of human devising that would even yet be set up to intervene between humanity and God and so annul the work of Christ. Human priesthoods, the veneration of intermediaries, the intercession of the saints—all with one sweep the book of Hebrews sets at nought.

Likewise the argument points up in striking fashion the glorious privileges of the Christian religion. When we understand what it means to have Christ as our great high priest, who could entertain for even a moment the base thought of forsaking Him?

So we see the two supreme blessings that come to Christians as a result of Jesus as our high priest. First, mercy—the bliss of sins forgiven. Then, grace for timely help—the power to meet temptation in the Christian life. So Christianity is not meant simply to be an easy way out of the sin problem. Forgiveness is not cheap with God. Unless Christianity leads to a new attitude to the temptations that Christians face, it falls short of the genuine thing.

Jesus and Aaron

As the comparison with Moses pointed up Jesus as faithful high priest, so that with Aaron highlights His mercy.

Hebrews 5:1-10 elaborates this point. The passage falls into two parts: verses 1-4, which describe the characteristics of the Aaronic high priest, and verses 5-10, which apply them (in part) to Christ as high priest.

Seven features emerge in the account of the Aaronic high priests:

1. "Chosen from among men" (verse 1), i.e., *human origin.*

2. "Appointed"; "called by God" (verses 1, 4), i.e., *divine choice.*

3. "Act on behalf of men" (verse 1), i.e., *representative service.*

4. "Offer gifts and sacrifices" (verse 1), i.e., *cultic service.*

5. "For sins" (verse 1), i.e., *atoning service.*

6. "Deal gently with the ignorant and wayward" (verse 2), i.e., *sympathetic service.*

7. "Offer sacrifice for his own sins" (verse 3), i.e., *sin-weakened service.*

This description of the earthly high priesthood is an idealized one. In no passage of the Old Testament do we find these points specifically set out, nor do we learn that sympathy was a requirement. Indeed, Israel's priests in the Old Testament were far from paragons of sympathy. While many high priests probably did "deal gently" with the sinners of ancient times, we know of others who certainly did not—the immoral and self-serving sons of Eli (see 1 Sam. 2:12-17); Pashhur, who opposed Jeremiah (see Jer. 20:1-6); and Amaziah, who could not bear to hear the rebuke of Amos (Amos 7:10-17). Nor could the apostle look to recent Jewish ecclesiastical history to prove his point. The Hasmonaeans, who held the high priestly office from 142 to 63 B.C., were embroiled in political concerns. They were secular rulers as well as religious leaders, while the Sadducees of the Gospel accounts opposed Jesus and coveted office.

The apostle does not develop a point-by-point comparison with Jesus as high priest in chapter 5:5-10. Only two out of the seven characteristics interest him—those of the divine appointment and sympathetic service. Just as no Aaronic priest could designate himself to the sacerdotal office, so the Son did not thrust Himself forward. He was appointed as priest by the divine word of Psalm 110:4: "Thou art a priest for ever, after the order of Melchizedek" (verse 4, K.J.V.). And just as the Aaronite priests were, according to the idealized account of Hebrews 5:1-4, beset with weakness and conscious of the fact, so the Son learned the lessons of frailty and dependence "in the days of his flesh."

The word translated "deal gently" in verse 2 is an interesting one. Literally it signifies "deal moderately." The setting is the high priest in relation to the age-old problem of human sin. On the one hand, since the priest stands in the presence of the Holy One, he must have a heightened awareness of the gravity of sin, of its opposition to the divine nature. Yet he should also remember humanity's weakness, which he can do only as he senses his own frailties. Aware of his own need, he may "deal moderately" with sinners as they come to him to mediate forgiveness. The various translations have endeavored to bring out the idea: "have compassion" (K.J.V.), "bear patiently" (N.E.B.), "deal sympathetically" (Phillips), and "can sympathise" (Jerusalem).

Yet while the apostle seeks to highlight the sympathetic high priesthood of Jesus here, he carefully avoids pressing the comparison with the Aaronites at the point of human weakness. He has told of the need of the Old Testament high priests to offer sacrifice for their own sins, but no such problem exists with Christ. Christ's sympathy arises rather out of His experience of learning obedience and being perfected through suffering.

Indeed, chapter 7:27, 28 specifically denies that Jesus would ever have any reason to sacrifice on His own behalf: "He has no need, like those high priests, to offer sacrifices daily, first for his own sins and then for those of the people; he did this once for all when he offered up himself. Indeed, the law appoints men in their weakness as high priests, but the word of the oath, which came later than the law, appoints a Son who has been made perfect for ever." We note here the contrast between "men in their weakness" and "a Son who has been made perfect for ever"—a direct summary of the argument of chapter 5:1-10.

As we look carefully at the reasoning of chapter 5:5,6 we discern a second point in which Christ as high priest breaks the Aaronite pattern of verses 1-4. The logic of these verses seems curiously distorted. In verse 4 the apostle has remarked that the priesthood is not self-conferred. So also with Christ. The Father appointed Him, as the apostle attempts to show, starting with verse 5. We would expect him to say, "So also Christ did not exalt himself to be made a high priest, but was appointed by him who said to him, 'Thou art a priest for ever, after the order of Melchizedek.' " Instead, we find, "So also Christ, . . . was appointed by him who said to him, 'Thou art my Son, today I have begotten thee,' as he says also in another place, 'Thou art a priest for ever, after the order of Melchizedek.' "

Clearly, the apostle sees divine Sonship (Ps. 2:7) to be as vital to Christ's priesthood as the declaration of Psalm 110:4. Indeed, the order of citing the passages indicates that the fact of Sonship is logically prior to the appointment as priest. That is, it is because Christ is *Son* that He may be designated Melchizedekian priest.

So now we see the correlation with the argument of

chapter 2:17, 18. There we noticed that Jesus *became* qualified to be high priest by becoming man. Here, the declaration of Sonship—a status, as we saw in chapter 2, which was His before the Incarnation—enables the word of appointment. This is exactly what chapter 7:28 says: "The word of the oath [that is, of Psalm 110:4—"The Lord has sworn and will not change his mind"] . . . appoints a Son [One who is Son, not *became* Son] who has been made perfect for ever [that is, by His human experiences of suffering, dependence, testing, and death]."

Thus, the second point of distinction between the Aaronite priests and Christ is in the status of each. The Old Testament high priests were taken "from among men" (chap. 5:1), but Christ is the Son who has been incarnated and so became qualified to be high priest.

A radically new concept of the priesthood of Jesus emerges. We see that the genuine Mediator between God and humanity without equivocation must be *both* God and man, without confusion, without dilution. And indeed, that is the case with our Lord. As Son, He embraces deity; as Son "made perfect," He grasps suffering, tempted, dependent humanity.

So there can ever be only one true High Priest. Only one Being in the universe can lay claim to both God and man in His own person. All the Old Testament priests but foreshadowed the Son, who would take our nature and our experiences to Himself and so be eternally qualified to mediate on our behalf.

Of the seven characteristics noted in chapter 5:1-4, then, the apostle directly applies two to Christ in verses 5-10 and denies two. The remaining three—the representative function, the cultic activity, and the atoning service—we find predicated of Him elsewhere. We may summarize our discussion of Christ and Aaron as follows:

AARON	CHRIST
Human origin	The Son "made perfect"
Divine appointment	Divine appointment

Representative service	Representative service
Cultic service	Cultic service
Atoning service	Atoning service
Sympathetic service	Sympathetic service
Sin-weakened service	Sinless service

The apostle, in the passage we have been considering, argues for the divine appointment of Christ as high priest by reference to the order of Melchizedek. He returns to the same idea in a sustained argument in chapters 6:19-7:28.

Christ and Melchizedek

The figure of Melchizedek has aroused speculation for more than two thousand years. The rabbis puzzled over the scant references to his person. Early Christians found themselves fascinated by his relation to Christ. Modern Christians debate the cryptic account of him in Hebrews.

But only five verses out of the entire Old Testament mention him—Genesis 14:17-20 and Psalm 110:4. Suddenly, without explanation, the person of Melchizedek appears amid the stories of the patriarchs. A contemporary of Abraham, Melchizedek *blesses* him. He is a priest long before the Lord proclaims the Jewish order of priesthood to Moses at Sinai. And long after the establishment of that priesthood, the voice of the psalmist heralds the rise of a new priest—one whose line will link with Melchizedek, not Aaron.

Melchizedek, in fact, was an embarrassment to some of the rabbis. In an attempt to establish him firmly in the line of Israel, some identified him with the patriarch Shem. (The genealogies permit it.) Another ingenious solution held that because Melchizedek blessed Abraham before blessing God (see Gen. 14:17-20) the priesthood was taken from him and given to Abraham.

If Christians had only the Old Testament references to Melchizedek, they probably would not show much interest in him. But he figures prominently in the New Testament, albeit only in one book—Hebrews. And here in chapter 7 we find perhaps the most puzzling words of the entire New Testament: "He is without father or mother or genealogy, and has neither beginning of days nor end of life, but resembling the Son of God he continues a priest for ever" (verse 3).

What sort of being is Melchizedek? A man from another planet? Christ coming down to earth in human form nearly two thousand years before Bethlehem? Or, as certain Adventists have maintained (and some even cite an apocryphal statement attributed to Ellen G. White), the Holy Spirit? No wonder the passing of the centuries has not diminished interest in the puzzle of Melchizedek.

Let us at the outset be clear on two matters.

First, *we completely miss the point of Hebrews if we focus our attention on Melchizedek instead of Christ.* The summary statement concerning Melchizedek ends with the assertion *"resembling* the Son of God he continues a priest for ever."* The priest-king of ancient Salem is chronologically prior to the incarnate Son, but theologically the Son is prior. Only on this basis can we account for the reasoning that would have otherwise been, as might be expected, "and the Son of God resembles his priesthood." Thus, only by considering the figure of Melchizedek in a subsidiary relationship to the priesthood of Christ can we rightly discern the apostle's intent.

A quick overview of the entire seventh chapter confirms our finding. We may break down the flow of thought into the following paragraphs:

Verses 1-3: A description of Melchizedek, who is likened to the Son of God.

Verses 4-10: Melchizedek shown to be greater than Levi, since Abraham paid tithe to and was blessed by him.

Verses 11-14: The prediction of a change in the law of the Levitical priesthood.

Verses 15-19: The new priesthood of Christ based on "indestructible life" and bringing full access to God.

Verses 20-22: The new priesthood confirmed by an oath.

Verses 23-25: The new priesthood confined to only one

priest, Jesus Christ.

Verses 26-28: The new priesthood has a sinless Son as priest.

The cryptic third verse and the convoluted reasoning of the chapter have led students of Hebrews to an undue concern with Melchizedek. But no more than Abraham or Levi is Melchizedek the center of the apostle's interest. In fact, the apostle does not mention him after verse 17.

Second, *we fail to understand the role of Melchizedek in the argument until we see the importance of Psalm 110:4 for the apostle.* Specifically, he does not launch upon an exposition of the Melchizedek passage of Genesis 14:17-20 and thereby move to an application to Christ. Rather, the prediction of a Messianic priesthood "after the order of Melchizedek" found in Psalm 110:4 leads him back to the Genesis account—the only other mention of Melchizedek in the Old Testament.

It is instructive to see the way in which he plays on Psalm 110:4 in the course of the sermon. The passage comes up over and over and is undoubtedly of key importance. He quotes it in full or in part, each time using it to give scriptural backing to the particular point he happens to be making:

1. Chapter 5:6. Quoted in full. The totality of the divine utterance indicates the divine appointment of the perfected Son to the high-priestly office (verse 10).

2. Chapter 6:20. The last part only—"priest for ever after the order of Melchizedek." The reference introduces the summary of Genesis 14:17-20 in Hebrews 7:1-3 and forms the basis for the entire discussion of Jesus as Melchizedekian high priest, which fills chapter 7.

3. Chapter 7:11. An allusion to Psalm 110:4. Here the author uses the prediction of the rise of another priesthood in the psalm to argue the *necessity* of a change in the Levitical priesthood.

4. Chapter 7:15-17. Again Psalm 110:4 is cited in full. The point here is that God has set forth a *new order* of priesthood, one that does not require physical descent from the tribe of Levi.

5. Chapter 7:20, 21. Only part of the divine words are quoted: "Thou are a priest for ever." Instead, the emphasis falls on the words of the *oath* that establish Him as a priest: "The Lord has sworn and will not change his mind."

6. Chapter 7:24. An allusion only, picking up the words of Psalm 110:4 that indicate Christ's *continuing* priesthood: a priest *"for ever."*

7. Chapter 7:28. A final allusion to Psalm 110:4, gathering together the ideas of divine appointment, divine oath, and eternal priesthood.

We may show the subtle shifts of emphasis in the use of Psalm 110:4 by italicizing the key words in each of the above occurrences:

1. Chapter 5:6: "a *priest* for ever."
2. Chapter 6:20: "the order of *Melchizedek.*"
3. Chapter 7:11: "the *order* of Melchizedek."
4. Chapter 7:15-17: "the *order of Melchizedek.*"
5. Chapter 7:20, 21: "the Lord has *sworn.*"
6. Chapter 7:24: "for *ever.*"
7. Chapter 7:28: "priest *appointed* by the words of the *oath* . . . is the Son . . . for *ever"* (N.E.B.).

As we look over chapter 7 we see that the overriding concern is the superiority of Jesus as high priest. In at least eight ways He is greater than the Levitical priests:

Because Melchizedek was greater than Abraham (and so greater than Levi), as shown by the blessing and receipt of tithe (verses 4-10);

Because the prediction of the new priesthood indicates inadequacy of the old (verse 11);

Because by Him comes "perfection" (verses 11, 19);

Because His priesthood is founded on an indestructible life, not on genealogy (verses 15-24);

Because it was made by a divine oath (verses 20-22);

Because He is one instead of many (verse 23);

Because of His sinless character (verses 26, 27);

Because He is Son (verse 28).

What a rich conception, then, is this idea of Hebrews— Jesus is our great high priest! At first sight so distant from our situation and problems, it is pregnant with spiritual meaning for Christians today. It places our religion squarely on an objective basis, apart from the winds and tempests of feeling. It tells us that God cares, that heaven is a welcome place, that we belong at the throne of grace.

Praise God for the gift of Jesus, our brother in the flesh, our risen Lord, our heavenly high priest!

Reality: The True Sanctuary

[Heb. 8:1-9:5]

Children dream of the land of make-believe, where they can fly, where animals talk, where the sun always shines, and where nothing grows old. But as they grow up, the unseen land evaporates in the harsh realities of human existence.

Adults also fantasize. Through soap operas and pulp magazines they identify with glamorous heiresses and handsome business magnates. They fly about in their private Lear jets and vacation in the South Pacific. But harsh reality is only the turn of the page or a turn of the knob away.

In the Bible, however, we learn about ultimate reality. The Scriptures assure us that, while this world is real and has come from the hand of God, it is not the ultimate. "Man shall not live by bread alone," said Jesus (Matt. 4:4). We were made for more than eating and drinking, marrying and giving in marriage, working and spending. God has made us for Himself—for a glorious endless future in His presence.

The book of Hebrews brings us face to face with that reality. After the apostle has elaborated in some detail the high priestly ministry of Jesus, and before he addresses our Lord's all-sufficient sacrifice for our sins, he pauses to discuss the locale of Christ's ministry—the heavenly sanctuary. That sanctuary, he says, is the true or genuine one—in contrast to the one made by Moses for the children of Israel.

As we take a brief look at this matter of the heavenly sanctuary we shall first notice a critical issue of interpretation, then discuss the significance of the idea to the Hebrew

Christians, and finally ascertain its meaning for us today.

The Interpretation of the Sanctuary Language in Hebrews

The language of the sanctuary permeates the reasoning of the book of Hebrews. Scholars, however, diverge widely as to its interpretation.

Is this language merely an illustration pointing to the reality accomplished by Christ on Calvary, or does it carry significance in its own right? That is, granted that the overall intent is to highlight what Christ has accomplished, what are we to make of "priests," "sanctuary," "blood," "offering," "purifying," and so on?

We can adjudicate the issue only by carefully analyzing the apostle's reasoning. We must ask ourselves the following questions:

1. How *serious* is the writer in employing the sanctuary language? Does he use it as a temporary expedient to be discarded when the language has served its purpose, or does the language retain its significance throughout?

2. Does the writer reveal, as it were, a "spiritualizing" purpose by clear indications that the sanctuary language is only a signpost to point to reality?

3. Is the cultic language *inherent* to the argument, or is it merely a vehicle for the argument? Here the underlying axioms of the arguments will be significant.

We may not dispense with the issue superficially. Only when we have considered the entire argument, with its shifts, turns, and ongoing development, can we venture upon an answer.

Obviously we have to consider at least three possible viewpoints. First, *a literalizing view*, which holds that the heavenly sanctuary and services are in all respects a replica of the earthly, right down to compartments, furniture, and so on. Second, *a spiritualizing view*, which maintains the sanctuary language merely illustrates the work of Christ. According to this view, we can set aside the language itself once we grasp that the author is merely using it to portray the all-sufficiency of Christ's sacrifice for us. Third, *an actualizing view*, which insists on a heavenly sanctuary, but not one that is a glorified copy of the earthly. While the work of Christ is indeed the chief point, the heavenly sanctuary guarantees the objective reality of what He is doing. This view delivers us from the extremes of literalizing and also from the perils of spiritualizing the argument of the book of Hebrews.

Although we are raising this critical issue of interpretation with regard to chapter 8 of the book, the matter embraces the discussion of the entire document. We can reach a satisfactory solution only as we take account of the entire book of Hebrews. Here is how I read the evidence.

With regard to the first line of interpretation—that the sanctuary language is to be understood as indicating a heavenly replica of the earthly—we need to bear in mind that the apostle reasons from both comparison and contrast. As we noted at the very outset, the author continually balances the old and the new. He argues that the old is good but that the new is better.

This line of reasoning extends to the discussion of the sanctuary itself. In chapter 9, verses 1-5, he gives a thumbnail sketch of the first sanctuary. However, he does not seem to be interested in discussing details of the earthly sanctuary. He cuts off the description quite brusquely with the words "Of these things we cannot now speak in detail." And when he talks of the heavenly sanctuary, as he does in chapter 8, he does not go into any detail about it. He simply calls it the true or genuine tent.

In chapter 8:5 we find three words used to describe the relationship between the earthly sanctuary and the heavenly: *hypodeigma*—signifying an outline or copy, or shadowy outline; *skia*—signifying a shadow, a pale reflection; *typos*—a type, pattern, model, figure, or copy, a stamp struck by a die.

The idea of correspondence of earthly temples to heavenly prototypes occurs in a variety of religions. At least as early as the Babylonian *Enuma Elish*, which dates from at least 500 years before the time of Moses, we encounter this concept. Likewise, we find in ancient literature correspondences of the king's house and the god's house, and earthly cities with heavenly models (for example, the cities of Nineveh, Asshur, and Sippar).

What, then, are we to make of Hebrews' description of the heavenly sanctuary? Probably that the heavenly sanctuary is the reality and that the earthly sanctuary was but a shadow of that reality. As a shadow points out an object, giving its outline but failing to supply details, so the earthly sanctuary limned the divine counterpart.

No earthly structure could adequately portray the heavenly temple. "The abiding place of the King of kings, where thousand thousands minister unto Him, and ten thousand times ten thousand stand before Him (Dan. 7:10); that temple, filled with the glory of the eternal throne, where seraphim, its shining guardians, veil their faces in adoration, could find, in the most magnificent structure ever reared by human hands, but a faint reflection of its vastness and glory."—*The Great Controversy*, p. 414.

Those scholars who favor the second line of interpretation—that the sanctuary language of Hebrews is meant only in a spiritualizing sense—often refer to the writings of Philo Judeaus. Philo uses some of the same terms as the book of Hebrews—*hypodeigma* and *skia*. But when Philo speaks of a heavenly sanctuary, the intended meaning is quite general: the heavenly sanctuary is the universe. His thought is thoroughly Platonic, with this earthly, sensory world standing over against the ideal world, which exists in the realm of pure thought.

But at several points the argument of the book of Hebrews parts company with Philo's Platonic world.

1. Plato's ideal world was not a place where anyone could enter—not even Jesus. It could be reached only by the intellect.

2. Plato's ideal world is timeless, but the apostle insists that Jesus, at a particular moment in time, entered the true tent. That is, he contrasts not merely an earthly copy and a

heavenly reality, but also two eras. We see this contrast made in sharp terms at chapter 10:1: "The law has but a *shadow of the good things to come.*" Here the earthly/heavenly contrast (shadow) is crossed by the temporal contrast of the old and the new.

3. In chapter 9:23 the apostle speaks of the necessity of purifying the heavenly realities. This idea is impossible on a Platonic model, and those scholars who have tried to argue the Philonic interpretation of Hebrews have found this particular verse an exceedingly hard nut to crack.

Further, as we follow the entire argument of the book of Hebrews, we do not find that the author moves away from the language of the sanctuary. From beginning to end he sets forth Jesus as high priest, one who ministers in the heavenly sanctuary. He does not give us a single clue that would suggest to us that the language of temples, sacrifices, priests, blood, and purification is something that we must transcend. To the contrary, this language *in itself* remains vital to the ongoing discussion.

In my judgment, therefore, the author of Hebrews intends us to understand his language of the sanctuary along the lines of the third interpretation suggested above. This language points to Jesus as the true high priest of an actual heavenly temple. However, we know very little concerning the details of His ministry in the temple. The earthly sanctuary with its furniture and ministries gives us hints about the heavenly—but only hints. The earthly was a shadow, not the reality itself.

The Meaning for the Hebrew Christians

Scholars have discovered evidence of considerable Jewish speculation concerning a heavenly sanctuary and liturgy. This specualtion dates from before and at the time of the writing of Hebrews.

In the Testament of Levi we read, "In it [the heavenly tabernacle] are the archangels, who minister and make propitiation to the Lord for all the sins of ignorance of the righteous; offering to the Lord a sweet-smelling savour, a reasonable and bloodless offering."

Similarly the Book of Jubilees has this: "And may the Lord give to thee . . . to serve in His sanctuary as the angels of the presence and as the holy ones."

The Testament of Dan calls for man to "draw near unto God and unto the angel that intercedeth for you, for he is a mediator between God and man."

Now we can better grasp the course of the argument concerning Christ as high priest. Against contemporary ideas of angelic ministry and mediatorial work in a heavenly sanctuary, the apostle affirms the vast superiority of the Son. Jesus alone is our high priest! Angels have a role to play in the divine purpose, but we must never place them alongside the one, eternal high priest.

Likewise with Melchizedek. A scroll discovered in Cave Number 4 at Qumran has a fair amount to say about him. The scroll is in a bad state of preservation, but it seems clear that the people who lived here by the Dead Sea associated Melchizedek with priestly activity in the heavenly sanctuary. The book of Hebrews rules out any such ideas, which may have been causing doubt among the apostle's own Christian readers. He emphasizes the uniqueness of Jesus. Melchizedek is but a curious figure out of the Old Testament, the record of whom forms a helpful point of departure to argue for the superlative qualities of the one, eternal, heavenly high priest.

Thus, in his discussion of the high priesthood of Jesus, the author of the book of Hebrews accomplishes two purposes. First, he corrects those ideas current among the Jews that would have exalted the ministry of angels and Melchizedek in the heavenly courts. Second, he points his readers to the magnificence of Jesus, the only true high priest, whose person and work far exceed that of Aaron and Melchizedek. Jesus ministers in the temple above, one more glorious than Solomon's Temple.

The Meaning for Us

The sanctuary doctrine has played a pivotal role in

Seventh-day Adventist history. Those critics both outside and within the church who have dubbed the doctrine a face-saving device and have called upon us to abandon it have failed to grasp its place in our history as well as our present experience.

The teaching was born out of the pain of bitter disappointment. It is the child of the blighted expectations of the thousands who waited all night on October 22, 1844, for the Lord to come to His sanctuary—the earth, as they understood it.

Out of the pain, out of the blasted hopes, out of the struggles to understand, came new light. The book of Hebrews played a decisive part, pointing out, as it does so clearly in chapter 8, that Christ is minister of the *heavenly* sanctuary. The Advent believers came to realize that Christ's cleansing of the sanctuary involved a heavenly work.

Many of the early believers in the second coming of Christ, of course, gave up the sanctuary doctrine. But for those who continued to study it and who came to find its meaning in heaven rather than on earth, the doctrine bore precious fruit. And it still speaks to us today.

1. It assures us that Jesus, our Creator and Redeemer, also is Lord of time. This conviction profoundly affects our view of the world and our place in it. It guarantees that human history, apparently chaotic and meaningless, is being guided toward a glorious goal by the Saviour. In the midst of terrorist bomb squads, organized crime, and the threat of nuclear holocaust, "He's got the whole world in His hands."

Adventists are people of hope. We do not deny this world—for our Lord created and redeemed it—but we "look for new heavens and a new earth, wherein dwelleth righteousness" (2 Peter 3:13, K.J.V.).

Jesus promised: " 'I will come again and will take you to myself, that where I am you may be also' " (John 14:3). As David Livingstone used to say, "He is a gentleman who keeps His word." The "blessed hope" of the church in all ages is guaranteed by that promise.

New Testament hope is not a blind optimism. Like faith and love, the other members of Paul's trilogy (1 Cor. 13:13), it is not in vain. It is as sure as the cross. It is as sure as Jesus, the Lord of time, our heavenly high priest.

2. It assures us that Jesus knows the future. The Biblical claim is both bold and breathtaking: "Behold, the former things have come to pass, and new things I now declare; before they spring forth I tell you of them" (Isa. 42:9). "The revelation of Jesus Christ, which God gave him to show to his servants what must soon take place; and he made it known by sending his angel to his servant John" (Rev. 1:1).

At the close of each year Jeane Dixon and other seers make their predictions for the ensuing twelve months. They usually bat about .500—which, given the generalized nature of most of their "prophecies," most well-informed people could equal if they put their minds to it.

The Bible also contains predictions—hundreds of them, and many long-term in nature. They are God's challenge to the skeptic and the infidel. God's knowledge of the future does not negate the part of human choice. Prophecy arises from the divine foreknowledge, not from His determining the course of events. Nor does God provide prophecy to satisfy curiosity seekers. Rather, as Jesus said, only after the event do God's people grasp the full intent of what He had predicted and so grow in faith (see John 14:29).

Adventists are a people of prophecy. Our roots are in the great lines of prediction in Daniel and Revelation—especially Daniel 2, 7, and 8, and Revelation 12-14. All these prophecies which compass in panoramic sweep the rise and fall of nations and the struggles of God's people, climax in the end-time. We believe that we now live in that end-time, when God will bring the reign of pain and evil to a close and make righteousness to flourish.

3. It assures us that Jesus is now our mediator and judge. The time prophecies of Daniel and Revelation—the 1260 days and the 2300 days (Dan. 7:25; 8:14; 9:24-27; Rev. 11:3; 12:14; 13:5)—play a decisive role in Adventism. Highlighted is the year 1844 as a turning point in divine history, when a heavenly work of judgment, prior to the Second Advent, began.

In this pre-Advent judgment (usually termed the "investigative judgment" and vividly described in Daniel 7:9-14, 26, 27) Jesus is our mediator and judge. Since God knows all things, the judgment does not convene for the purpose of revealing to Him who are righteous. Rather, it demonstrates His justice and righteousness to the universe.

The thought that we are *now* in the time of God's judgment invests the present with awe and expectation.

With awe, because *our* lives lie open to the heavenly audit. That audit reveals our relationship to Christ, who alone is our hope.

Ellen White has described the solemnity of our times: "In the typical service, when the work of atonement was performed by the high priest in the most holy place of the earthly sanctuary, the people were required to afflict their souls before God, and confess their sins, that they might be atoned for and blotted out. Will any less be required of us in this antitypical day of atonement, when Christ in the sanctuary above is pleading in behalf of His people, and the final, irrevocable decision is to be pronounced upon every case?"—*Selected Messages*, book 1, p. 125.

But also with expectation, because the judgment assures us that soon the reign of evil will come to an end. Soon there will be no more Bhopal tragedies, with two thousand killed and many more poisoned by methyl isocyanate gas. Soon there will be no more twisted bodies and retarded brains as a result of Ethiopian famine. Soon there will be no more nuclear madness, terrorist madness, Mafia madness.

Soon, from the sanctuary, Jesus will come back to us!

Power in the Blood

[Heb. 9:6-10:18]

"To remove the cross from the Christian would be like blotting the sun from the sky," says Ellen White. "The cross brings us near to God, reconciling us to Him. With the relenting compassion of a father's love, Jehovah looks upon the suffering that His Son endured in order to save the race from eternal death, and accepts us in the Beloved."—*The Acts of the Apostles*, p. 209.

We have come to the theological climax of the book of Hebrews. In chapters 9:6-10:18 we find a sustained, closely reasoned argument that takes us into the very heart of God. And at that heart we find a cross.

In several respects Jesus was unlike any other human baby. Apart from the fact that He was the God-man and that He bore no propensities to sin, He was born to die. We read references throughout His ministry to "his hour" or "my hour," indicating that it lay just ahead. He knew where the road of God's will was leading Him. He knew, especially as He started out on that last, long journey to Jerusalem, what lay at its end. He knew that in the heart of God, in the plan of salvation devised before the world began, there was a cross.

The passage before us is exceedingly rich. In a short chapter we cannot begin to plumb its depths. We simply will take up four aspects, treating them only briefly as space allows. First we shall meditate on the mystery of God's way of saving humanity. Then we shall pause to think of the desperate need of salvation brought by sin. Our third aspect will discuss the key term *blood* that we find throughout this chapter. Finally we shall look at issues of special interest to

Seventh-day Adventists in this passage.

The Mystery of God's Salvation

How God saves humanity will be the song and science of the redeemed throughout the ceaseless ages of eternity. Although God has made the way so simple that even a child may enter it and so that the wayfaring man need not err therein, only He knows its full dimensions. It should not surprise us if some aspects of the plan remain mysterious for us. After all, it is *His* way of salvation. He does not call upon us to understand it but rather to accept it. In Christianity salvation comes by faith, not by intellectual gymnastics.

Consider, for instance, that imposing but mysterious text which seems to lie at the heart of the argument of Hebrews 9:6-10:18: "Indeed, under the law almost everything is purified with blood, and without the shedding of blood there is no forgiveness of sins" (Heb. 9:22).

"Without the shedding of blood there is no forgiveness of sins"—here we encounter a spiritual axiom. Remember geometry classes and statements such as "a straight line is the shortest distance between two points"? Axioms, by their very nature, cannot be proved. They are the foundation of all subsequent reasoning. They are law, tied to the nature of the universe itself. Two plus two equals four—always has done so and always will.

And God tells us that without the shedding of blood there can be no putting away of the sin problem. There it is, a spiritual axiom. We may struggle with it, wrestle to grasp why it should be so, but God simply says, "This is the way of salvation."

Human reasoning is apt to rise up and say, Surely the cross was but one of several options open to God. Since God is infinite, would He not have before Him an infinite number of ways of dealing with the new situation caused by sin?

And other questions arise. Some of them stretch our moral reasoning.

Take the sacrificial system, for instance. According to

God's directions, a person who committed sin was to take an animal—a sheep, an ox, or a bullock—bring it before the altar, confess over it his sins, and then cut the throat of the beast. This was the way of salvation in the Old Testament. If you like, it was the way of righteousness by faith. As we well know, the whole system was a teaching device that pointed to Jesus Christ.

But reason asks, Of what use were these multiplied deaths of animals? Suppose in my anger I rise up and kill another person. Now a dead man lies on the ground. What shall I do to make right what I have done—shall I now slay a sheep? Ten sheep? A hundred sheep? A thousand sheep? Can the blood of animals take away my sin? Under the sacrificial system we have not only a dead man but also dead animals!

Yes, human reasoning may raise questions such as these. But God provided the sacrificial system. All the ordinances laid down in the book of Leviticus came from Him. The individual who, conscious of sin, desired to find forgiveness followed the provision made by God.

Then there is the substitutionary aspect. No court of law in our land will permit someone else to assume the punishment of a guilty man or woman. If I have killed a man, I must stand in the dock and hear sentence pronounced upon me. My wife, my son, my daughter, my father or mother, my best friend—no one can take my place. Though someone may wish to come forward to die in my place—and that surely would be a very rare thing—the law simply does not permit it.

But God's plan of salvation transcends human law systems. At its heart is the cross of Jesus Christ. He was treated as we deserve that we might be treated as He deserves. He is the sinless one, the spotless lamb of God, the one altogether lovely. We are wretched in our sinfulness, without hope and without redeeming virtue in ourselves. But He assumes our guilt and our penalty so that we might assume His righteousness and His eternal life.

"Without the shedding of blood there is no forgiveness of

sins." The words captivate us; they are haunting, mysterious. They take us back in time to those councils made in heaven, when the members of the Holy Trinity made provision to meet the yet-to-come terrible emergency of sin. And these words tell us that that provision centered in a cross.

Our Desperate Need

Nowhere does the Bible set forth a complete explanation of the plan of salvation. It makes very clear the way to salvation, but it gives only hints as to the manner in which the plan of salvation operates—its internal logic. Rather than a complete theological scheme of salvation, we find in the New Testament a series of models or metaphors that set out in various ways the human predicament. And likewise they show the way in which Christ by His death meets our desperate need.

Probably the most familiar model is the law court. Though it is very old, it still has power to grip us. None of us likes having to appear in court—even to answer a speeding violation. And, should we be required to go to court, we want to get back outside in the fresh air of freedom just as soon as possible!

Now, the court model or metaphor stands behind one of the most familiar terms used to describe salvation—*justification*, which suggests acquittal. Accused of terrible crimes, we stand in the dock, and although we are guilty, we go out as free men and women because of Jesus' sacrificial death.

But the justification model is only one of a series that we find in the New Testament. The Biblical writers did not invent a new vocabulary (if they had, of course, they would have been speaking gibberish). Rather, they took over words and concepts from everyday life and applied them to our spiritual situation. The following table sets out the basic life situation behind some of the most common New Testament words that point to our salvation.

Basic Thrust (life situation)	Problem	Solution
Rescue from danger	Life endangered	Salvation
Financial transactions	Debt requires payment	Forgiveness
Personal relations	Estrangement	Reconciliation
Marketplace (buying/selling)	Sold	Redemption
Law court	Guilt	Justification
Liberation from bondage	Slavery	Liberated
Cosmic conflict	Demonic rule	Christ the victor
Search	Lost	Found
Sacrificial system	Sacrifice required	Expiation of sin

Thus, when a Christian says, "Jesus saved me," his words mean that Jesus *rescued* him from grave peril. "Jesus forgave my sins" suggests that Christ has paid up his debt. (Hence Matthew's form of the Lord's Prayer: "Forgive us our debts.")

In the book of Hebrews, especially in chapters 9 and 10, the terrible problem that we call sin is set out in terms of defilement. And the solution provided by Christ's work corresponds to the problem: Christ brings purification.

"For if the sprinkling of defiled persons with the blood of goats and bulls and with the ashes of a heifer sanctifies for the *purification* of the flesh, how much more shall the blood of Christ, who through the eternal Spirit offered himself without blemish to God, *purify* your conscience from dead works to serve the living God" (chap. 9:13, 14).

"Indeed, under the law almost everything is *purified* with blood, and without the shedding of blood there is no forgiveness of sins" (verse 22).

"Thus it was necessary for the copies of the heavenly things to be *purified* with these rites, but the heavenly things themselves with better sacrifices than these" (verse 23).

"For since the law has but a shadow of the good things to come instead of the true form of these realities, it can never, by the same sacrifices which are continually offered year after year, make perfect those who draw near. Otherwise, would they not have ceased to be offered? If the worshipers had once been *cleansed*, they would no longer have any consciousness of sin" (chap. 10:1, 2).

"Let us draw near with a true heart in full assurance of faith, with our hearts sprinkled *clean* from an evil conscience and our bodies *washed* with pure water" (verse 22).

This language of defilement and purification is a fundamental expression of our terrible need before God. It is ancient language, but amazingly modern; for our need continues.

In *The Symbolism of Evil*, Paul Ricoeur has analyzed the language of confession. Studying the various religions of the world, he finds at the heart of such language the symbol of dirt. The prime statement of the human condition as man sees himself is this: we are dirty, defiled. We should not think that ideas of defilement belong to a primitive type of religious mentality, one that fails to distinguish ritual from moral questions. Pollution of the body is but part of a deeper, internal problem. The spirit of man, as it were, has been stained and needs to be washed clean.

Defilement is like a contagion. It may lurk in the most innocent-looking places; the mere touch of a drinking vessel, a stone, a particular foodstuff, a certain mountain may transmit it. In the story of the world's religions, every conceivable object, whether animate or inanimate, personal or impersonal, has been viewed as a source of pollution. What is most precious in one culture may be most dangerous in another.

These ideas of defilement and purification are still with us. They continually surface in modern language. Why do we refer to "dirty politics," "dark deeds," and "filthy stories"? The American passion for cleanliness has roots that lie deeper than concern for good hygiene. The old adage "cleanliness is next to Godliness" strikes a response in the deep subconscious. It is amazing how often the symbolism of dirt and cleanliness come to our lips, whether in "That was a dirty trick" or the command to "come clean!"

Thus, when the writer of Hebrews sets forth the human

problem in terms of defilement and Christ's solution in terms of purification, he touches deep springs within the heart of every one of us.

The "Blood" of Christ

Among the theological richness of Hebrews 9:1 to 10:18, the leading term is *blood.* It occurs no fewer than thirteen times in this passage.

In three key places in the passage we find the argument clinched by the expression "not without blood." At chapter 9:7 the high priest enters the Most Holy Place of the heavenly sanctuary "not without taking blood." The first covenant was inaugurated "not . . . without blood" (verse 18). And according to the axiom of verse 22, there can be no putting away of sin "without the shedding of blood."

Chapter 9, verses 13 and 14 summarize the argument of the passage: "For if the sprinkling of defiled persons with the blood of goats and bulls and with the ashes of a heifer sanctifies for the purification of the flesh, how much more shall the blood of Christ, who through the eternal Spirit offered himself without blemish to God, purify your conscience from dead works to serve the living God."

The reasoning here is clearly from the lesser to the greater. Animal blood purifies the outward person, reasons the apostle, but *how much more* will the blood of Christ purify the whole being! Christ's sacrifice deals not with cermonial aspects, but enters into the very consciousness of humanity. It purges the guilt and the shame, taking away the nagging sense that we are defiled and out of harmony with God.

So we find a series of positive statements about Christ's blood:

Chapter 9:12—Christ enters once for all through His own blood to the heavenly sanctuary. This is the access theme. By His death Christ has abolished all barriers between God and man.

Chapter 9:14—Christ's blood purifies the conscience (consciousness).

Chapter 10:19—We have boldness to enter the Most Holy Place through His blood.

Chapter 10:29—His is the blood of the new covenant (verse 20 also).

Chapter 13:12—Christ sanctifies (sets apart for a holy use) His followers "through his own blood."

Throughout the book of Hebrews a leading term is *better*. Thus, we have noticed the better revelation of chapter 1:1-4. Christ's name is better than that of the angels (verses 5-14). He is a better leader (chaps. 3:1-4:13). His high priestly ministry is better than Aaron's (chap. 5:1-10). The order of His priesthood belongs to that of Melchizedek (chap. 7:1-28). His is a better sanctuary (chap. 8:1-5). He mediates a better covenant (verses 6-13). And here in chapters 9:6-10:18, the climax of the theology centers in "better blood."

In this passage we do not find any negative connotation attached to the blood of Christ. His blood does not defile. Rather, it provides the answer to the desperate problem of sin. Blood is the blessed medium provided by God. It brings thorough purification.

Precisely what is intended by the expression "blood of Christ"? Is the term to be equated with His death?

Indeed, the thrust of the passage suggests that the blood of Christ signifies more than merely His death. Blood represents a powerful medium, a cleansing agent, one that is efficacious to take away the terrible contagion of sin. Blood represents Christ's life poured out in death. It is our hope and salvation.

Dr. Paul Brand in a recent book coauthored with Philip Yancey, *In His Image* (Zondervan, 1984), makes some enlightening observations concerning blood. The entire book is a reflection on the church as the body of Christ, with analogies taken from the human body.

"Some years ago an epidemic of measles struck Vellore and one of my daughters had a severe attack. We knew she would recover, but our other infant daughter, Estelle, was dangerously vulnerable because of her age. When the pediatrician explained our need for convalescent serum, word went around Vellore that the Brands needed the 'blood of an overcomer.' We did not actually use those words, but we called for someone who had contracted measles and had overcome it. Serum from such a person would protect our little girl.

"It was no use finding somebody who had conquered chicken pox or had recovered from a broken leg. Such people, albeit healthy, could not give the specific help we needed to overcome measles. We needed someone who had experienced measles and had defeated that disease. We located such a person, withdrew some of his blood, let the cells settle out, and injected the convalescent serum. Equipped with 'borrowed' antibodies, our daughter fought off the disease successfully. The serum gave her body enough time to manufacture her own antibodies. She overcame measles not by her own resistance or vitality, but as a result of a battle that had taken place previously within someone else.

"There is a sense in which a person's blood becomes more valuable and potent as that person prevails in numerous battles with outside invaders. After antibodies have locked away the secret of defeating each disease, a second infection of the same type will normally do no harm. A protected person has 'wise blood,' to use a term Flannery O'Connor originated. Could this process cast light on the description of Christ being 'made perfect through suffering' (Heb. 2:10)? Recall the just-quoted passage from Hebrews: 'Because he himself suffered when he was tempted, he is able to help those who are being tempted' (2:18). And again, 'We do not have a high priest who is unable to sympathize with our weaknesses, but we have one who has been tempted in every way, just as we are—yet was without sin' (4:15)."—Pages 94, 95.

For our terrible problem of sin God has provided the plan of salvation! For our dirt and defilement—Christ's blood!

The Day of Atonement in the Book of Hebrews

For the final section of this chapter we will take up an issue of keen interest to many Adventists. Precisely what role does the Day of Atonement play in the thought of the apostle?

The Day of Atonement references (e.g., chaps. 9:7, 25; 10:1) have deeply disturbed some Seventh-day Adventist students of Hebrews. They have reasoned that Hebrews parallels the Old Testament Yom Kippur ceremonies with the work of Christ on Calvary, thereby indicating that Christ fulfilled His ministry in the Most Holy Place of the heavenly sanctuary at Calvary. Such a conclusion, of course, makes shipwreck of the traditional Adventist view of a "first apartment" work up to 1844, with the "second apartment" function of judgment—the antitype of the Old Testament Day of Atonement—commencing in 1844. Not surprisingly, several students of Hebrews, among whom A. F. Ballenger is best known, have eventually parted company with the SDA Church because of such interpretation.

The problem and their reaction to it illustrates well a basic principle of Biblical interpretation: *We must put to the text only questions appropriate to its context.* The text is not a computer, as it were, into which we may feed any theological and spiritual inquiries that come into our minds, press the keys, and extract the answers. Each Biblical document is a product of time and place. While the Holy Spirit inspired the Bible writers—and so Scripture has an enduring significance—each author addresses a particular group of people. The Word of God is always at the same time the word of man. We may not bypass the historical conditionality of the text. Only as we understand the original readers and their concerns may we rightly interpret it.

The fundamental misunderstanding of Hebrews by Ballenger and others lies in putting the wrong questions to the text. In the Hebrews the apostle does *not* deal with the work of Christ in the heavenly tabernacle from a *time* perspective. What he is concerned with is one supreme idea—the *all-sufficiency of His death*. He contrasts the Old Testament sacrifices with the one superlative Sacrifice. To do this, he takes the high point of the Old Testament religious year—Yom Kippur—and argues that even on this day the sacrifices did not resolve the sin problem, as shown by the annual reenactment of Yom Kippur. The highest point of the Old Testament cultic year could not purge sin away! Obviously, if the Day of Atonement services were inadequate, how much more were all other sacrifices.

Christ's own blood, however, accomplished the putting away of sins *with finality*. No more need of sacrifice remains. That once-for-all event surpassed and superceded all the Yom Kippurs of the old cultus. It not only provided decisive purification—even of the uneasy "conscience"—but it flung open the Temple to all. Through His sacrifice we may come with absolute confidence into the heavenly tabernacle.

Thus, the Day of Atonement is an important point in the apostle's argument in the book of Hebrews. However, it is by no means the main argument that he uses with regard to sacrifice. In fact, the Day of Atonement occurs as but *one* of a series of references he makes to sacrifice. Throughout the book the apostle talks about the daily sacrifices of the Old Testament, the sacrifices of the covenant, the red heifer, and so on. He does not lift out the Day of Atonement for exclusive attention. No, his leading idea is "better blood." Christ's blood, His sacrifice, is better than all other sacrifices, the Day of Atonement included. To suggest that the Day of Atonement forms the basis of the argument is to misread the thrust of the apostle's writing.

So far as providing of a sacrifice was concerned, Calvary was the antitype of the Yom Kippur sacrifice, just as Christ is the antitype of all Old Testament sacrifices. But the Old Testament Day of Atonement had several aspects: a time aspect (a particular day of the year), a particular sacrifice (the Lord's goat), and a specific ritual (the ministry in the Most Holy Place was performed only then). As we seek to move from the Old Testament type to understand the antitypical Day of Atonement, we should keep these three aspects in view. Because Calvary is the antitype of the *sacrificial* aspect of the Day of Atonement, we should not necessarily conclude that Calvary is the antitype of the other aspects as well.

Thus, on the basis of the Scriptures Seventh-day Adventists believe that the antitype of the *time* aspect came in 1844, when Christ entered upon His work of judgment in the heavenly sanctuary. This work, which will bring to a close the agelong controversy between good and evil, corresponds with the special ritual of the Day of Atonement—the Most Holy Place ministry. And just as in the type the final putting away of sin was portrayed by sending the living goat, Azazel, into the wilderness, so the antitype of the Day of Atonement extends to the final eradication of sin and sinners and the restoration of a new heavens and a new earth.

It is clear, therefore, that the argument of the book of Hebrews does not deny the Adventist sanctuary doctrine. On the basis of texts such as chapter 9:23 we may say that Hebrews allows for this doctrine—although it does not develop it. The thrust of Hebrews is looking back to Calvary, rather than looking forward to the work of judgment.

In summary, what have we learned in Hebrews 9:1-10:18 about the sacrifice of Christ? Two things principally.

First, Christ's act solves the sin problem. We don't have to strive and stretch, to hunger and thirst, to press and prevail, in a frantic, frenzied, and futile effort to find cleansing from our sins. By one sacrifice for all time God has utterly dealt with sin. Nothing we might do can add to the sacrifice or diminish from it. The blood of Christ gives us absolute confidence for the putting away of our sins. Says Ellen White: "Our great High Priest completed the sacrificial offering of Himself when He suffered without the gate. Then a perfect atonement was made for the sins of the people. Jesus is our Advocate, our High Priest, our Intercessor. Our present position therefore is like that of the Israelites, standing in the outer court, waiting and looking for that blessed hope, the glorious appearing of our Lord and Saviour Jesus Christ."—Manuscript 128, 1897.

Second, Calvary assures us of our full access to the presence of God. No matter who we might be, we *belong* in Jesus Christ. The gates of the Temple stand flung open. All who believe may enter—not cringing, but boldly. We come with bodies washed and "hearts sprinkled clean from an evil conscience," as brothers and sisters of the Son incarnate, who died on our behalf.

Awaiting Christ's Return

[Heb. 10:19-35]

In 1914 an expedition led by Ernest Shackleton set out from England. The party hoped to make the first crossing of the continent of Antarctica. It would sail to the Weddell Sea and traverse the continent via the South Pole, meeting the sea at McMurdo Sound.

With high hopes the party set out in the *Endurance.* But the expedition was doomed from the outset: Pack ice closed around the ship before the explorers could even reach the Antarctica continent. For nine months the *Endurance* creaked and groaned under the pressure of the ice, and then at last it split in two. What a dilemma! Shackleton and his men were at the end of the earth, trapped in a wilderness of ice.

For five months the members of Shackleton's expedition drifted around on large ice floes. Then, with the help of small boats they had salvaged from the *Endurance*, they made their way to Elephant Island. Don't be misled by the name of that island—not even a rat lives on it. It is a windswept desert of ice and snow. The nearest human habitation was eight hundred miles away on the island of South Georgia. But the wildest sea in the world lay between—and Shackleton had only an open whale boat to attempt the crossing.

Still, that small boat was the party's only hope. Taking five men, Shackleton set out. As he waved Goodbye to the forlorn party on Elephant Island, he wondered if he would ever see them again. And they wondered too. On Shackleton rested their hopes of rescue.

The voyage in the open whale boat was one of the epic crossings of the twentieth century. Despite the mountainous waves with which the tiny vessel had to contend, the party made landfall on the island of South Georgia. However, they landed on the side of the island opposite from the British whaling settlement. Since the seas were so rough and the party so exhausted already, Shackleton decided to attempt to cross overland to the whaling base. Taking with him two of his companions who were fit enough for the journey, he set out. South Georgia, in the news in more recent times as the site of the first battle between the British and the Argentinians in the Falklands War, is very rugged. In fact, no one had ever traversed it before. But at last they reached the whaling station. Now the world was alerted to the fate of the party of men isolated on Elephant Island.

Soon a rescue attempt was organized. The first attempt failed. The pack ice closed in, and the rescue ship could not find a way through to Elephant Island. It had to turn back. A second attempt was organized. But again the ice closed in around the island, and the ship turned back. A third attempt—and once again the ice was the victor.

Only after four rescue attempts could Shackleton find a way through to Elephant Island. As he approached that wilderness of snow and ice, he wondered what he would find. Would anyone still be alive after those months of waiting? Would there be, perhaps, a few survivors gone mad with the silence and the waiting?

Shackleton found every man alive, in good condition, and in good spirits. How had they survived? The secret lay in the leadership of the man Shackleton had left in charge. Every day he would say to his men, "Get ready, boys. The boss may come back today."

And so every day they got ready. Every day they prepared themselves. Every day they watched. Every day they waited. And despite the long silence, despite the long odds, one day Shackleton did come back.

We Christians also live in a time of waiting. Nearly two

thousand years ago our Leader promised His people, " 'I will come again.' " Every writer of the New Testament believed that promise. The New Testament is a book of unbounded confidence. Its message centers upon two poles in history—the first coming of Jesus and His second coming. The first coming guarantees the second. *Because* He once came and lived among us, died our death on Calvary's tree, and won the victory, His return is absolutely certain.

Hebrews 9:28 puts it well: "So Christ, having been offered once to bear the sins of many, will appear a second time, not to deal with sin but to save those who are eagerly waiting for him." Note how it combines the two comings.

But already in the first century some of those who professed the name of Jesus had grown weary. They had expected Jesus' promise to return to be fulfilled quickly, so as the years passed they began to waver, began to doubt. Their spiritual conflict grew deeper as scoffers arose who mocked, " 'Where is the promise of his coming? For ever since the fathers fell asleep, all things have continued as they were from the beginning of creation' " (2 Peter 3:4).

The seeming delay in the return of Jesus bothered some of the Hebrew Christians, too. The passages covered by the tenth chapter of Hebrews leave us in no doubt.

Some of the readers were wavering, doubting God's promise (verse 23).

Some had grown careless in church attendance (verse 25).

Some had gone so far as to sin deliberately, flagrantly (verses 26, 27).

Some were forgetting the hard struggles they had had in former days, when they were publicly exposed to abuse, affliction, suffering, and plundering of their property (verses 32-34).

Some were throwing away their confidence (verse 35).

And so the apostle affirms the hope of the Second Coming: " 'For yet a little while, and the coming one shall come and shall not tarry; but my righteous one shall live by faith, and if he shrinks back, my soul has no pleasure in him.' But we are not of those who shrink back and are destroyed, but of those who have faith and keep their souls" (verses 37-39).

The Hebrews' problem is our problem too. If some of them began to doubt even in the first century, how much more likely are we to doubt after nearly two thousand years!

The Seventh-day Adventist Church was born under the banner of the "blessed hope." Our pioneers first expected that Christ would return in person on October 22, 1844. They were wrong, of course, and were bitterly disappointed; but they did not give up hope. They trusted the promises of His Word, so they went back to that Word to search for answers. They concluded that they had been wrong in their expectation of Christ's return to earth in 1844. However, the date was significant because it marked the commencement of His work of judgment in the heavenly sanctuary. With that work under way, they knew that His return could not much longer be delayed.

But the pioneers are all gone. Joseph Bates, James White, Ellen White, John Nevins Andrews, Uriah Smith—all that godly band are long since gone.

Some of us have been Adventists for many years. Some of us grew up in the church and can look back on twenty, thirty, forty, fifty, perhaps even sixty, years of "blessed hoping." How fast the years have flown—years that so far have failed to bring the Saviour back to us.

Some Adventists spend considerable effort in trying to find a theological answer to the seeming delay of Jesus' return. They have suggested a variety of reasons. As interesting as their proposed solutions have been, we cannot take them up here. Instead, we will place the emphasis where both the Bible and Ellen White's writings put it—in personal preparation for the Second Coming.

The key question for every Adventist is this: How shall I wait? How can I be among those who do not turn back but who hold their confidence firm unto the end, who "have faith and keep their souls" (verse 39)? How can I be like those described by Jesus, our returning Lord, in Luke 12:35-40: " 'Let your loins be girded and your lamps burning, and be like men who are waiting for their master to come home from the marriage feast, so that they may open to him at once when he comes and knocks. Blessed are those servants whom the master finds awake when he comes; truly, I say to you, he will gird himself and have them sit at table, and he will come and serve them. If he comes in the second watch, or in the third, and finds them so, blessed are those servants! But know this, that if the householder had known at what hour the thief was coming, he would not have left his house to be broken into. You also must be ready; for the Son of man is coming at an unexpected hour' "?

In the remainder of this chapter I shall consider briefly various responses to the question How shall I wait? And I shall look at the answer given in Hebrews 10:19-35.

How Shall We Wait?

I have observed various reactions to the apparent delay in the return of Jesus.

1. Eschatological burnout. Burnout is a term that has become more and more familiar to people in our day. After years of hard work, a man quits his office and takes to the road. The reason? Burnout. He is tired of the routine, tired of the pressure. He also may leave his wife and family, change his lifestyle, look for a totally new line of work. He is tired of the hassle and weary with the routine.

Some people are burned out with regard to the hope of the Second Coming. Long ago many of the mainline churches set aside this doctrine. They concluded that because so many years have passed, the promise of Christ's return simply has to be wrong.

Some Adventists are also burned out. Some of them heard preachers and evangelists many years ago proclaim the signs of the times and predict Christ would come within six months, a year, perhaps five years at the most. Maybe they heard such sermons several times. But the years have gone by. Some Adventists have grown old with waiting. And now they have given up. Some no longer come to church. Some attend church, but when they hear talk of the Second Coming, they quietly "turn off" inside. They have suffered burnout.

And there are the critics of Adventism, of course. They chide us: "Why don't you Adventists give up? Look, more than 140 years have passed since 1844. You were wrong. Why don't you admit it?"

But I'm not giving up the hope of the Second Coming. If Adventists have a problem here, all the New Testament Christians had the same problem! The promise of the Second Coming stems from Jesus Himself. It is guaranteed by His Word. I know Jesus; He is the one who has forgiven my sins. He promised that if I would come confessing, He would grant me His redemption. I took Him at His word, and He kept His promise. He also promised, "I will come again." He has not yet come, but He surely will some day.

2. *A state of excitement.* In July, 1984, I received an interesting letter from a man in the Northwest. The letter arrived just a few days before the Democratic Party was to choose its Presidential candidate at its convention in San Francisco. The letter consisted of a series of calculations based on the Greek text of Revelation 17. Its conclusions were as follows: "The next President after Reagan will continue a short space (Rev. 17:10). This will be Walter Mondale, unless Reagan dies before he finishes his term on January 20, 1985. Mondale's successor will be his Vice President. . . . Evidently Kennedy will be Vice President to Walter Mondale in January of 1985."

If the good brother in the Northwest had waited just a few days, he need not have mailed that letter! As the world soon knew, the Democrats did elect Walter Mondale as their Presidential candidate, but they turned to Geraldine Ferraro as the Vice Presidential nominee. And Mondale went down to resounding defeat to Ronald Reagan in the November elections.

Every time a Presidential election year rolls around, people rise up to make similar predictions. Others, of course, do not wait until election years before drawing up scenarios of the end of all things!

Nor are such calculations confined to Seventh-day Adventists. Hal Lindsey's book *The Late Great Planet Earth* has sold close to 20 million copies, and it has been translated into many languages. He has made a series of predictions, some of which already have been falsified by history. But Lindsey continues to forecast the end of all things. For some years he has been pointing to the eighties as a time of significant developments that involve entities such as the European Common Market.

He is not alone in the evangelical world. Tim LaHaye, for instance, recently released *The Coming Peace in the Middle East* (Zondervan, 1984). This book paints a scenario of Armageddon as occurring in our day.

Is this the way we should wait for Jesus to come? Should we scan the newspaper headlines or raid the evening television news in order to try to establish a particular time for His return?

Among His very last counsels to His followers, Jesus gave a series of predictions about the Second Coming (Matthew 24, Mark 13, Luke 21). However, the signs given by Jesus are quite general in nature. In His wisdom the Lord did not lay down a detailed timetable of events in order that we would know precisely how many years or months might remain before His return.

Rather, His words indicate that only after events have come to pass do we realize the full meaning of His predictions (see John 14:29). This course is no doubt for our best good. Many of us simply could not handle a detailed knowledge of the future. We would either collapse with fear or be so self-confident that we would put off the needed preparation and lose our eternal salvation.

The Lord doesn't want us to be continually in a state of superexcitement about something we read in the newspaper or hear on the news. We should be alert and watchful, but it is not given to us to know precisely the time of the Lord's return.

In fact, signs of the end are all around us, but they do not make the headlines because they are not of a sensational nature. Changes in society happen slowly and therefore usually do not attract the attention of the media. What are such signs? The decline of Protestantism. The resurgence of the Papacy. The renewal of interest in religion (not necessarily in Christianity). The preponderance of church-state issues, especially in the United States. Modern people's fascination with the occult.

All these are signs of building momentum on a worldwide basis toward the last events in the great controversy between good and evil. They tell us that the end is near, that Jesus' promise to return surely must be fulfilled soon.

In a sermon preached at Lansing, Michigan, on September 5, 1891, Ellen White gave specific instruction on how we should wait for the Lord to return. Specifically warning us against trying to calculate the precise time of the Lord's coming, she said: "The times and the seasons God has put in His own power. And why has not God given us this knowledge? Because we would not make a right use of it if He did. A condition of things would result from this knowledge among our people that would greatly retard the work of God in preparing a people to stand in the great day that is to come. We are not to live upon time excitement. We are not to be engrossed with speculations in regard to the times and the seasons which God has not revealed. Jesus has told His disciples to 'watch,' but not for a definite time. His followers are to be in the position of those who are listening for the order of their Captain; they are to watch, wait, pray, and work, as they approach the time for the coming of the Lord; but no one will be able to predict just when that time will come; for 'of that day and hour knoweth no man.' You will not be able to say that He will come in one, two, or five years, neither are you to put off His coming by stating that it may not be for ten or twenty years."—*Selected Messages*, book 1, p. 189.

Rather than being engrossed in time speculations, we

should make the most of every flying moment. We should redeem the time, sharing with others the good news of the dying, risen, and returning Saviour and growing in the graces of the Christian life.

The Counsel of the Book of Hebrews

Hebrews 10:19-39 shows us how to live in the waiting time.

1. *Confident living.* Verse 19 tells us, "We have confidence to enter the sanctuary by the blood of Jesus, " while verse 22 admonishes, "Let us draw near with a true heart in full assurance of faith."

God has called us to assurance, not doubt. He has given us the blessed assurance that He is on our side, that He wants us to be with Him forever. "He who did not spare his own Son but gave him up for us all, will he not also give us all things with him?" (Rom. 8:32).

What more could God have done? Before the world was, before sin ever made its ugly entrance, He devised the plan for our redemption. In the fullness of time He sent the only-begotten Son, Jesus, the fairest among ten thousand. God Himself took upon Himself our flesh and blood to live with us, to suffer with us, to struggle with us, to overcome for us, and at last to die in our place.

And now, having broken the bonds of death, He reigns as king, intercedes as high priest, and sits as judge in the heavenly sanctuary. Heaven is a welcome place. Heaven is our home.

We need not come into His presence with cringing and fear, with spiritual hat in hand. We *belong!* We are His sons and daughters. He has broken down the barriers, opened a new and living way through the Incarnation. There is no need to offer animals, no need to offer incense, no need to be in fear and doubt. He is our great high priest.

Confident Christian living is not presumption. It does not take sin lightly. It ever remembers that sin sent the spotless Son of God to Calvary's cross. It will never joke about sin. It will never take the Saviour's name lightly.

Rather, it is distressed by sin. It seeks not to justify one's self, but comes confessing. It does not claim perfection of the flesh, realizing our weakness and the deceptiveness of sin.

So our blessed assurance means that we are delivered on the one hand from the fear that God has rejected us, and on the other hand from a careless, presumptuous form of "cheap grace."

2. *A bold confession.* "Let us hold fast the confession of our hope without wavering, for he who promised is faithful," admonishes the apostle (verse 23).

Ours is a world of waverers. Relativism has taken over the thinking of most men and women—old standards and mores have been thrown out the window, and conduct is subject to the whims and passions of the fleeting moment.

In such a time as this we must stand firm for the Lord. Between the people of God and the people of the evil one is drawn a clear line. Christian identity must not be compromised to the world. We can have no truck with the ways and devices of the enemy. We are children of the King, sons and daughters bought with the blood of Prince Emmanuel.

Let us remind ourselves who we are. Let us stand true to the name that we bear. Let the world know that we are Christians—and especially by our love!

3. *Considering one another.* "Let us consider how to stir up one another to love and good works," the apostle goes on (verse 24).

Some Christians stir up one another—but not to good works! They are continually on the lookout for faults and flaws. Eagerly they compile statistics of supposed mistakes in others. Or, to use Paul's language in the book of Galatians, they are like cannibals, feasting on the flesh of their fellows.

But if we have gained a concept of the beauty of the life of Jesus, if our hearts have been strangely warmed in contemplation of Calvary, if we marvel day by day at God's love in providing our great High Priest in the heavenly courts—if we are conscious of such blessings, we will be conscious of one another. We will realize how weak, how needy, we are—*I am*—and therefore how dependent on the grace of God. And out of that realization will grow a tender concern, a love for other souls, a deep pain when someone leaves the Christian way, a sensitivity to the cares and hurts of others. Also we will show an appreciation for our fellows, a quickness to commend (praise is not flattery), a readiness to help, and genuine pleasure in the success and advance of others.

Life in the world is like a pyramid. Men and women claw and scratch their way to the top. Often they trample on their fellows, because the higher they rise, the fewer they see beneath them. But Jesus inverts the pyramid of life. In His kingdom he is greatest who serves; he is the chief who is the slave of all. The goal is not to trample on one's fellows, but to carry them on one's shoulders.

And at the apex of this inverted pyramid we find Jesus Christ. On His shoulders He bears the whole world.

4. *Joyful church attendance.* "Not neglecting to meet together, as is the habit of some, but encouraging one another, and all the more as you see the Day drawing near," says the apostle (verse 25).

Attendance at church is not simply an option for the Christian. As Christians, we are members of the body of Christ. We are not alone. Just as the hand, eye, or foot cannot exist apart from the other members, so we cannot "go it alone."

This is an age of unbelief. By getting up on Sabbath morning and going to the worship services, we exercise the will to believe. We refuse to drift along with the common crowd, floating in the lake of doubt. We rise up to hear the preaching of the Word, to share the fellowship of the saints, to strengthen and be strengthened.

Yes, it is possible to worship out in nature. It is possible to go aside quietly on one's own for study and prayer. But such times should be exceptions. As Christians, *because* we are Christians, we belong in church on Sabbath morning. And absenting one's self from church is a clear evidence that spiritual life has started on a toboggan slide.

How, then, shall we wait? We will wait confidently,

boldly.

How, then, shall we wait? We will wait in hope, knowing that the One who promised to come back is the One who already has demonstrated His promises a thousand times in our experience.

How, then, shall we wait? We will stand fast in the Christian way, unmoved by the currents that swirl about us. We will boldly confess to the world our risen Saviour who serves in the courts above and who soon will pierce the clouds.

How, then, shall we wait? We will tell the good news near and far—to our neighbors, to our friends, to our loved ones. We will build up our fellow saints and let the world know that we are Christians.

How, then, shall we wait? We will exercise the will to believe by getting up and going to church Sabbath by Sabbath, no matter how hot or how cold it may be, no matter how inviting bed may seem.

And one day soon "the coming one shall come and shall not tarry" (verse 37)!

Looking Unto Jesus

[Heb. 11:1-12:2]

Many years ago in Egypt two parties were embroiled in dispute both over property. To prove her case to the judge, the rightful owner gathered together her documents and sent them to the court by the hand of a trusted servant. In order to keep them secure, she put them in an earthen vessel. The servant stopped off at an inn along the way—and that night the inn burned down. We do not know what happened to the slave or to the woman's claim on the property, but the documents the servant was carrying remained in the earthen pot buried under ash and under the sands of Egypt. Almost two thousand years passed by until in our times the archeologist's spade uncovered the pot. There in the vessel lay the woman's letter to the judge. In it she set out her claim to the property. And there was the legal document that she had sent to establish her claim—the title deed.

This incident from long ago is of great interest to us as we study the apostle's teaching about faith in the book of Hebrews. We are familiar with the description of faith in chapter 11:1: "Now faith is the substance of things hoped for, the evidence of things not seen" (K.J.V.). These words, however, are better known than they are understood. Just what did the apostle mean by faith's being the *substance* of things hoped for?

This is where the archeologist's discovery from ancient Egypt greatly helps us. In setting out her claim to the property, the woman said that she was enclosing her *hypostasis*. And what did she enclose? The title deed. Now, in Hebrews 11:1, the Greek word translated "substance" in the King James Version is that same word—*hypostasis*. That is, we can translate Hebrews 11:1 like this: "Faith is the *title deed* of things hoped for, the evidence of things not seen."

We all know the value and importance of title deeds. Without a title deed to a house or a car, any one of us will have great difficulty in establishing ownership. But with such a title deed, and if that deed is indeed genuine, all arguments cease.

Faith, says the apostle, is the title deed to the things for which we hope. Suppose you have a great aunt Harriet. You've not seen her for years, perhaps had pretty well forgotten that she existed. One day you receive a letter in the mail from a legal office. Aunt Harriet's lawyer informs you that your great aunt has gone to her rest and that in her will she has left you her property in Hawaii. In a state of excitement you rush to the lawyer's office. You wonder if his letter can really be true. But the lawyer takes out the title deed to Aunt Harriet's property and puts it in your hand. The property is yours because you now hold the title deed—even though you've never been to Hawaii and seen the property.

That is the way with faith. The book of Hebrews reminds us that the unseen things, the eternal things, are the truly real ones. The apostle admonishes us to look not at the things that are seen, because they are temporal, but at the things that are not seen, which are eternal. And he tells us that faith is the title deed to those things. Although we have never been to heaven, although we have never seen the heavenly realities with our mortal eyes, they are real by faith, and in fact they are ours—because if we have faith, we have the title deed to them. They are as real as that property in Hawaii that we have never seen, and our claim to them is even more sure.

What a marvelous conception! How this simple illustration, made clear to us by the recent discovery from ancient Egypt, brings encouragement to the Christian! Truly the Christian life is life in another dimension, a dimension that the non-Christian cannot begin to understand.

The Twin Elements of Faith

Hebrews 11:1 is not, strictly speaking, a definition of faith. Rather, it is a description, setting forth two elements that comprise faith.

Faith, in fact, is a relational term. It can never be reduced to a definition. To define it is to lose it. In essence faith is a relationship of trust, the giving of one's self completely to the Lord. This is why Paul in Romans 14 contrasts faith with doubting and concludes that whatever is outside the circle of faith is sin. The Christian lives within the circle of faith—in the circle of a trusting relationship. We know our Master, and we know that He knows us. We trust Him in the darkness as well as in the light, just as did Job, who could say when his whole world collapsed, "Though he slay me, yet will I trust in him" (Job 13:15, K.J.V.).

In the descriptive analysis of faith in Hebrews 11:1 elements of time and space intersect. Faith is the title deed to things hoped for. That is, it is future directed. It looks beyond this present world to eternal realities. Faith longs and hopes for the day when God's promises will be realized fully for the believer. Faith also is the evidence of things not seen. It knows that *already* the unseen world exists, that the heavenly realities for which we long and toward which we strive have been provided by God and will come into our view in His good time.

In Hebrews 11:6 we see this blending of the two elements of faith: "And without faith it is impossible to please him. For whoever would draw near to God must believe that he exists and that he rewards those who seek him." The one who comes to God must believe that He is—that is, must see the unseen. But he also must believe that God is the *rewarder* of those who earnestly seek Him. The future will bring a realization of God's promises.

Hebrews 11, surely one of the most famous chapters of the Bible, sets forth a series of examples of men and women from ancient times. As we analyze this long list, we realize that every example illustrates the opening verse of the chapter. Some of the examples illustrate the first part of the verse—the element of hope. Other examples illustrate the second part of the verse—the element of the unseen. In some examples the two elements blend, as in Hebrews 11:6.

Thus Noah was warned of things that had never been seen on earth before (verse 7). Likewise Abraham obeyed God, going out to a place he had not seen (verse 8). But Abraham also looked forward to the city that has foundations, whose builder and maker is God—that is, he believed that God would fulfill his hope. Likewise Sarah, already far beyond the time of bearing children, believed that God would keep His promise of an heir (verse 11).

So we read this about the men and women of faith in ancient times: "These all died in faith, not having received what was promised, but having seen it and greeted it from afar, and having acknowledged that they were strangers and exiles on the earth" (verse 13). Here in this verse we see the twin elements coming to the fore. The ancient worthies lived in hope, seeing through the eye of faith the better land that God had provided for them.

We find these same elements in the illustration of Moses given in verses 23-28. Moses, says the apostle, considered abuse suffered for Christ greater wealth than the treasures of Egypt, for he looked to God's reward (verse 26). He was confident of his master; faith was his title deed to the things to come. By faith he left Egypt, not being afraid of the king's anger, for he endured because he saw Him who is invisible (verse 27). The eye of faith looked beyond the assembled might of Pharaoh's army (the horses and the chariots and the weapons of war), beyond the defenseless condition of the children of Israel (a motley band of slaves). Faith saw, like Elisha, angel hosts surrounding God's people. Those who are for us are more than those against us.

As we consider the description and examples of faith given in the book of Hebrews, we realize that the concept of faith held by many Christians is inadequate. Some Christians associate faith with that moment of decision when we give our hearts to the Master. Or they think of faith in terms of particular problem situations in life when they are not sure what they should do or where they should turn, but nevertheless decide to step out "in faith."

These situations—coming to Christ initially and meeting life's difficulties—certainly are valid examples of faith. However, the book of Hebrews would tell us that faith involves far more than these. Faith is not something to be confined to particular moments in Christian experience. Rather, faith is an *ongoing* relationship with the Lord. It is a life of continuing trust, of continuing obedience, of continuing hoping, of continuing confidence in the presence of the Lord, of continuing looking to the unseen world, of continuing holding in our hand the title deed to the eternal realities.

Jesus, the Author and Perfecter of Faith

The chapter divisions, like the verse divisions, of the Scriptures are not inspired. They were added only in the Middle Ages. The chapter break between Hebrews 11 and Hebrews 12 is especially unfortunate. In Hebrews 11 the apostle has given us a long list of men and women of faith, but he has left the supreme illustration—Jesus—till last. "Therefore, since we are surrounded by so great a cloud of witnesses, let us also lay aside every weight, and sin which clings so closely, and let us run with perseverance the race that is set before us, looking to Jesus the pioneer and perfecter of our faith, who for the joy that was set before him endured the cross, despising the shame, and is seated at the right hand of the throne of God" (chap. 12:1, 2).

The picture is remarkably contemporary. We see the stadium, packed with spectators in the stands. We see the arena, laid out for the track and field events. We see the runners, laying aside all encumbrances and lining up as they await the starter's gun.

We are all runners in the race of life. Although in this life we already receive marvelous blessings as Christians, the best is yet to be. In this life we live by hope, by faith, as the gospel comes to us as promise. That is why faith is really faithfulness.

In this race of life everyone who finishes is a winner. Not just the place getters, not just the first thousand or five thousand—everyone who completes the course receives the prize. To finish is to win.

And at the end of the course, standing behind the finishing tape, is Jesus. He is urging us on. He has run this course already and finished it. He, the one who is fully God, became fully human and entered into our experiences. He knows what the race is like. He knows its struggles, its fatigue, its aches and pains as we labor up Heartbreak Hill. That is why He can be not merely the author of our faith, but also its finisher.

So as we run this race we must keep our eyes fixed on Him. We should not look around to the stands, even though they are packed with the spectators—probably the men and women of faith already mentioned in chapter 11. Nor are we to look back, remembering that, as Jesus Himself said, " 'no one who puts his hand to the plow and looks back, is fit for the kingdom of God' " (Luke 9:62). Nor should we look within ourselves, because our hearts are deceitful and desperately wicked. Looking at ourselves, we easily grow complacent and self-confident, or conversely, become discouraged and think we can never make it. No, we must keep our eyes fixed on Jesus. Fix them every day on Jesus. Fix them firmly on Jesus. Keep them fixed on Jesus.

The 1954 British Empire Games, held in Vancouver, British Columbia, provided a remarkable illustration of Hebrews 12:1, 2. The mile race held there is considered to be one of the greatest races, perhaps the greatest race, of all time. It pitted the two fastest men in the world over one mile—Roger Bannister and John Landy.

For decades runners had set the goal of the four-minute mile. They practiced and strove and thrust their bodies forward as their times drew closer and closer to the magic mark. But no one could break the four-minute barrier, and physicians began to say that it was beyond the ability of the human body to run a mile in four minutes. Roger Bannister, a medical student in England, didn't believe that. He applied medical science to the science of running as he practiced for the mile. And then one day in the spring of 1954 he did the impossible—he ran a mile in less than four minutes.

The sporting world went wild, but within a few weeks it had something else to shout about. Down in Melbourne, Australia, a dark-haired schoolteacher named John Landy became the second man in history to run a four-minute mile—and his time was faster than Bannister's.

So everybody began to ask: Who is the faster runner, Bannister or Landy? How can these two four-minute milers be brought together to compete?

And so to the Vancouver games, held in August of that year. I was not present at those games, but I have seen a film of the mile race. It is enormously exciting—and it runs for just four minutes!

Following his usual practice, Landy started fast. Unlike most runners, Landy's approach was to move to the head of the pack early and by the sheer power of his physique to outlast the other runners who would reserve strength for a final thrust at the tape.

The race was clearly between Bannister and Landy. Soon the other runners were dropping back, leaving Landy out in front, and Bannister well behind him.

At the end of each quarter mile the times were announced, and with each announcement the stands rocked. Landy and Bannister were setting a blazing pace, one that would surely set a new world record. But who would get to the tape first?

So the runners came to the final lap, the final quarter mile. Landy was in front, ahead of Bannister, as he had been throughout the race. Ahead of him stretched the tape, looming closer and closer. Somewhere behind him was Bannister.

And then a deafening roar arose in the stands. Landy knew what it meant: Bannister was making his last desperate effort to catch Landy before the tape.

The tape was getting closer and closer, and the roar louder and louder. Landy knew that Bannister in his last great effort was catching up. But where was he?

The film shows it. Before the tape Landy turned his head so he could see just where Bannister was. And Bannister, seizing the psychological moment, threw himself past Landy on the other side and just beat him to the tape.

This famous race, the "miracle mile," is enshrined in stone in Vancouver. Go to the city and you will see the two runners—one turning his head as the other thrusts himself by toward the tape.

As runners in the race of life, we are to keep our eyes fixed on Jesus. He who has begun a good thing in us will carry it forward to completion. He will present us faultless before His presence with eternal glory. He, the author of our faith, is also its finisher.

Mountain, Camp, and Shepherd

[Heb. 12:3-13:25]

We now come to the close of the book of Hebrews. We have worked our way through the carefully wrought theological argument. We have taken heed to the warnings of Hebrews, the strongest in all of Scripture. We have been inspired by the men and women of faith set forth in chapter 11. Above all, we have seen Jesus, the author and finisher of our faith, the heavenly high priest, our sinless sacrifice, and our coming king. Could these last two chapters of the book hold anything more for us?

In fact, most preachers and students of Hebrews pass over chapters 12 and 13. They concentrate on the theology of Hebrews or they expatiate on the practical examples of faith in chapter 11. One would almost gain the idea that Hebrews 12 and 13 were an appendage to the book. But that is far from the truth of the matter.

As we suggested in our opening remarks about the book of Hebrews, the apostle's concern is primarily pastoral. He himself describes the document as "a word of exhortation" (chap. 13:22). With all its complexities, the theological argument in its final analysis is designed to serve a practical purpose—to help rejuvenate the spiritual condition of the Hebrews Christians. So it is not at all surprising that the final words of the book of Hebrews should be practical in focus.

As we look over Hebrews 12 and 13 we see a variety of exhortations. We read about Christian discipline—the Lord's disciplining of His children. We hear warnings of falling away like Esau. We find encouragement to persevere in well-doing. We hear counsels concerning marriage, hospitality, and false teachings. In the main, the instruction is abbreviated and varied.

However, three passages stand out in this presentation: chapters 12:18-24, 13:10-13, and 13:20, 21. These passages in turn group themselves around three dramatic symbols—the mountain, the camp, and the shepherd.

The Mountain

Hebrews 12:18-24 is one of the most vivid in all Scripture. "For you have not come to what may be touched, a blazing fire, and darkness, and gloom, and a tempest, and the sound of a trumpet, and a voice whose words made the hearers entreat that no further messages be spoken to them. For they could not endure the order that was given, 'If even a beast touches the mountain, it shall be stoned.' Indeed, so terrifying was the sight that Moses said, 'I tremble with fear.' But you have come to Mount Zion and to the city of the living God, the heavenly Jerusalem, and to innumerable angels in festal gathering, and to the assembly of the first-born who are enrolled in heaven, and to a judge who is God of all, and to the spirits of just men made perfect, and to Jesus, the mediator of a new covenant, and to the sprinkled blood that speaks more graciously than the blood of Abel."

The passage falls into two distinct parts—verses 18-21, which deal with Mount Sinai, and verses 22-24, which describe the heavenly Mount Zion, the New Jerusalem. The contrasts are strong and inescapable. Sinai is the place of fire, darkness, gloom, whirlwind, and trumpet. It is the mountain that may not be touched, the mountain from whose summit thunder terrifying words that make the hearers quake. Even beasts that stray onto the mountain will be destroyed.

But the heavenly Jerusalem is just the opposite. It is the city of access, where multitudes of angels gather in joyous convocation. In it the saved of all ages will walk the streets of gold, without fear of each other or fear of their Lord. It is the place where Jesus is the mediator, and His blood—the blood of the new covenant—speaks peace and welcome to all who enter in.

As we read this dramatic description, two questions arise:

1. Is this contrast between the Old and the New Testament a fair one?

After all, Sinai *was* the high point of Old Testament religion. It was the capstone to the deliverance experience of the Exodus; the Jews ever after looked back to this theophany as the most dramatic manifestation of God in their midst. God gave the law at Sinai—the Ten Commandments, written with His own hand, immutable, eternal.

Furthermore, Old Testament religion was not something only of fear and trembling, of touch not and keep out. Think of the passages of Deuteronomy where God's gracious calling of His people and His going forth to forgive them and provide for them is set forth in terms matched only by the New Testament. Think of the psalms of praise and joy. Think of Psalm 23, the shepherd psalm. Think of Psalm 137, written by the Israelites in Babylonian captivity: "By the waters of Babylon, there we sat down and wept, when we remembered Zion" (verse 1). Zion, earthly Jerusalem, was a city of longing for the Jews.

We can understand Hebrews 12:18-24 only in the light of the apostle's entire development in the book. In our opening remarks about the document we stressed that one of the critical areas of interpretation is the balance between the old and the new. It is easy to collapse the new into the old, as though the coming of Jesus and His sacrificial death on Calvary did not make any real difference in salvation history. On the other hand, it is easy to denigrate the Old Testament, setting forth the New in such a way that the Old appears primitive, second-rate. Throughout the book of Hebrews the apostle carefully sets the New over against the Old. He makes very clear that the Old is not bad. It came from God. But at the same time he leaves us in no doubt that the New is *final*. It is the fulfillment of all that the Old promised and foreshadowed. Without the New the Old is a truncated pyramid, a torso, an unfinished edifice.

This balancing of the Old and New was critical for the readers to understand. As we have seen, many of them were tempted to fall back into Judaism. With Christianity still regarded as an illegal sect, and with the attraction of the Temple and its services, they could easily drift back to the old ways. This is why the book of Hebrews sets out in magnificent fashion the glory of the Christian religion. It argues that with Jesus comes *finality*. He is the perfect priest (in fact, the only true priest). He is the perfect sacrifice. His is the perfect (the real) temple.

Further, by faith in Him every Christian has access to the heavenly temple. Under the old dispensation only the priests could enter the sanctuary, and only the high priest could appear before the symbol of God's presence in the Most Holy Place—and that only once a year, on the Day of Atonement. But by His blood Jesus has opened a new and living way into the very throne room of God. Every son and daughter of Adam, no matter how insignificant in the eyes of the world, may approach boldly to the throne of grace. They need no mediator. They need no animal sacrifice. The blood of Jesus is sufficient. It has broken down all barriers between God and man.

This is what the colorful passage, Hebrews 12:18-24, is telling us.

2. How can the apostle say that we *already have come* to the heavenly Jerusalem?

By faith. We saw in chapter 11 that faith is the title deed to things hoped for; it is the evidence of the unseen. Faith is like a pair of spectacles that God provides. We put on these spectacles, and the things of earth grow strangely dim. We look beyond the glitter and the tinsel of this world's passing pleasures and peer into eternal reality.

Throughout the New Testament "the already" is balanced by the "not yet." For instance, John tells us that we already *have* eternal life (John 5:24), but he speaks about the resurrection of the righteous at the last day when they enter upon the eternal glory (verse 25). Likewise, Jesus proclaims the kingdom of heaven: " 'Repent, for the kingdom of heaven is at hand' " (Matt. 4:17). In the Sermon on the Mount He commences:" 'Blessed are the poor in spirit, for theirs *is* the kingdom of heaven' " (chap. 5:3). But He also tells parables of the kingdom, such as the illustration of the sheep and the goats in Matthew 25, which make clear that the righteous enter into the reward of the kingdom of heaven only at the Second Coming. That is, from Jesus' own words the kingdom of heaven already is present in some sense, but at the same time it awaits its full manifestation in the future.

So it is with the book of Hebrews. We are now citizens of the heavenly kingdom; we now have a great High Priest; He now ministers in the heavenly courts for us. But we are strangers and pilgrims on this earth. We are bound for the better land, which we see now only by faith. But one day we will see that land; one day faith will turn to sight. One day the "not yet" will merge with the "already." Then we shall see our Master face to face.

The Camp

Hebrews 13:10-13 tells us: "We have an altar from which those who serve the tent have no right to eat. For the bodies of those animals whose blood is brought into the sanctuary by the high priest as a sacrifice for sin are burned outside the camp. So Jesus also suffered outside the gate in order to sanctify the people through his own blood. Therefore let us go forth to him outside the camp, and bear the abuse he endured."

Notice the elements of this striking passage.

1. *"We have an altar."* This statement reminds us of previous "we have" statements of the book of Hebrews: chapter 4:14—"We have a great high priest who has passed through the heavens"; chapter 8:1—"We have such a high priest, one who is seated at the right hand of the throne of the Majesty in heaven."

We see in this statement the apostle's confidence in Christ. He reminds us of the fact of the new priesthood, the fact of the new sacrificial system—and of its superiority to the old.

We also sense the conflict of church and synagogue, of Christ and the Temple. The apostle's illustration has its roots in the Levitical regulation concerning the sacrifice of animals. Parts of these animals were to be eaten by the priests. But by that same regulation all who were not priests were denied access to these portions. Now behold the glory of Calvary! Calvary is the new altar, and one does not have to be born a Levitical priest to eat of its sacrifices!

"We have an altar." The words are striking, even defiant. They open a window on that world of the New Testament, that world where Christians were just a small, despised sect, the Johnny-come-lately in the gallery of religions.

I wonder if we can still say it today and say it with their assurance—"We have an altar." Are Jesus Christ and His death precious in our sight? Today we do not face the opposition of Judaism and the scorn of the Roman world. But ours is a world that profanes the sacred, that puts its confidence in the here and the now, in the tangible and the pleasures of the flying moment.

"We have an altar"! Are we quite *sure* about that? Can we proclaim it with the same boldness as the book of Hebrews?

2. *"Outside the camp."* This phrase occurs many times in the first five books of the Bible. "Outside the camp" was the place to which lepers were banished. "Outside the camp" was the place where criminals roamed. "Outside the camp" was the site for the execution of wrongdoers. "Outside the camp" was uncleanness, the cutting off from the Temple and the holy people.

And now comes the startling statement—Jesus suffered "outside the gate"! And as His followers, we are to go with Him outside the camp! What can it mean?

Think of Calvary. Jesus, God's perfect sacrifice for sin, was not slain on the altar of burnt offering in the Jerusalem Temple. He did not die within the city walls. He was taken outside the gate, outside the sacred grounds to the place of execution. He died "outside the camp" on Golgotha's hill, the place of the skull. Jesus, God's perfect sacrifice for sin, died on unhallowed ground, in an unclean place, in a profane place.

Think of the implications! Because Jesus erected His cross in a profane place, He left no hill or valley, no city or village, no spot on Planet Earth that does not belong to Him. We should not and cannot say that Jesus is to be found only within the walls of the church. We cannot confine Jesus to this place or to that place, to this monastery or to that dedicated ground. Every place is His, for He won the whole world to Himself when He went outside the gate to die in our stead.

We live in a world that is becoming increasingly secularized. Science with its technology goes from strength to strength. The role of religion seems to shrink every year. For more and more people the bottom line in life is determined not by the Bible or by the preacher, but by empirical data and technology.

We can notice various responses as people try to relate the sacred to the profane. First, there are those who seek to secularize the sacred. They would make all things common, breaking down the dividing wall between the holy and the common. Second, there are those who seek to live, as it were, in two compartments. One part of them lives in the realm of the sacred when they go to church. The rest of the time they live in the realm of the profane as they go about the business and pleasure of daily life.

The book of Hebrews presents a radical alternative to both of these approaches, however. It also would break down the dividing wall between the sacred and the profane, but not at the expense of the sacred! It would tell the Christian that the whole world is to be won for Christ, that He is the Lord of this world, that He *belongs* in every place.

I think it is dangerous and un-Biblical to try to live in two compartments. For the Christian, all of life is tinted with the beauty of Jesus. All of life, whether it be our work or our play, is to be consecrated to Him. The alternative suggested by Hebrews involves more than just listening to "sacred music" on Sabbath and "secular music" after the sun sets. We honor the Lord of the Sabbath by keeping His day holy, but we honor Him on the other six days also by the way in which we go about our work and conduct ourselves in our homes.

In the fourth century a strange movement swept across the face of Christendom. Men and women left homes, jobs, wives, and children. Some fled to the desert, perching on the top of rocks or pillars for years on end, like Simeon Stylites. They exposed themselves to the burning sun and the cold night wind. They starved themselves. They even spurned washing.

The Sicilian monk Conon existed for thirty years on only one meal a week. Another devotee, Adolus, slept only the last three hours before dawn. Another of these fellows spent the night on a crag so that if he fell asleep he would fall to his death. Another would not lie down, but slept standing in his cell. Another ate nothing cooked by fire for seven years; as a result his bones stood out. And it is said of Simeon Stylites that he dropped vermin as he walked.

What madness was this? These people thought they were pleasing God. They thought they were following the way of holiness. They thought that God wanted them to flee from this world.

They should have read Hebrews 13:10-13. The place of the Christian in the world is right there—in the world! We are to go outside the camp, following where Jesus has led the way and claiming the entire world for Him in the name of His victorious cross. Not in convents, not in monasteries, not in Adventist ghettos, but outside the camp—that is where Jesus leads us!

The Shepherd

And so to the final passage and picture in Hebrews 12 and 13: "Now may the God of peace who brought again from the dead our Lord Jesus, the great shepherd of the sheep, by the blood of the eternal covenant, equip you with everything good that you may do his will, working in you that which is pleasing in his sight, through Jesus Christ; to whom be glory for ever and ever" (chap. 13:20, 21).

Most people are surprised to learn that this is the only

reference to the resurrection of Jesus in the book of Hebrews. That is all the more surprising when we realize how the preaching of the resurrection dominates the book of Acts. Indeed, the fact of the resurrection underlies many of the letters of the New Testament.

But our presentation of the book of Hebrews already has prepared us for this verse. Hebrews is the great book of the high priesthood of Jesus. Hebrews pictures Jesus as ministering in the heavenly sanctuary, the real temple. It continually lifts our eyes to those unseen, eternal verities. And therefore it *assumes* the resurrection of Jesus. If He in fact is ministering in the courts above, then He has burst through Joseph's tomb.

And here in this lovely benediction we meet again and for the last time that blending of theology and practical concern which characterizes the book of Hebrews.

We meet the theology in the expression "by the blood of the eternal covenant." This succinct phrase sums up the long, convoluted, intricate, beautifully wrought argument of Hebrews 8 through 10. In a few words it reminds us of all that has gone before about the sacrifice of Jesus—its all-sufficient character, its sinlessness, its power to purge our conscience, the access it provides to the very presence of God. Praise the God of peace for the blood of the eternal covenant!

And we meet again the practical concern of the apostle. "May the God of peace," he says, "equip you with everything good that you may do his will, working in you that which is pleasing in his sight, through Jesus Christ." For him theology is not an abstract idea, not something for professors and seminary students merely to haggle over. Theology issues in life—a life well pleasing to God. Those who *know* Jesus as their high priest, those who have come under the blood of the eternal covenant, can never be the same again. They are the sheep led by a Shepherd. They follow Him, content to listen to His voice and to follow where He leads. In all their ways they seek to please Him.

Some Christians become concerned with talk of Christian assurance. They fear that such talk will lead people into carelessness, into presuming upon the grace of Christ. They would prefer a presentation of Christianity that leaves hearers in a state of suspended uncertainty about their standing with God.

On the other hand, some Christians so speak of the blood of Christ and the riches of His grace, so speak of the "already," that one wonders if there is a "not yet" that will someday come to fruition. And one fears lest their assurance turn into a heady confidence that may lead them to make light of sin.

The book of Hebrews guides us between the Scylla of uncertainty and the Charybdis of false confidence. Anchoring our faith firmly in the person and work of the magnificent Jesus, it leads us on in blessed assurance. As we climb the hill that leads to heaven, the book of Hebrews reminds us that we are pilgrims and strangers on this earth—and that the best is yet to be.

For Further Study

I f you enjoyed *Blessed Assurance*, you'll want to read *In Absolute Confidence*, also by William G. Johnsson. Dealing specifically with Hebrews, Dr. Johnsson isolates the leading ideas of the book and sets out clearly the "message" of Hebrews. And, as he has done in *Blessed Assurance*, he shows the significance of Hebrews for Christians living today. The book is scholarly, but written in a simple and uncluttered manner, so that any Bible student may profit from it. Available now at your Adventist Book Center.

IN ABSOLUTE
CONFIDENCE
The Book of Hebrews Speaks to Our Day
William G. Johnsson